Shadows of the Future

Utopianism and Communitarianism
Lyman Tower Sargent and Gregory Claeys
Series Editors

Utopianism and Communitarianism
Lyman Tower Sargent and Gregory Claeys, Series Editors

This series offers historical and contemporary analyses of utopian literature, communal studies, utopian social theory, broad themes such as the treatment of women in these traditions, and new editions of fictional works of lasting value for both a general and scholarly audience.

Other titles in the series include:

Shadows of the Future

H. G. Wells, Science Fiction, and Prophecy

Patrick Parrinder

SYRACUSE UNIVERSITY PRESS

Published in the United States by Syracuse University Press,
Syracuse, New York 13244-5160, by arrangement with
Liverpool University Press, Liverpool, United Kingdom.

Library of Congress Cataloging-in-Publication Data
Parrinder, Patrick
    Shadows of the future : H.G. Wells, science fiction, and
prophecy / Patrick Parrinder.
        p. cm.—(Utopianism and communitarianism)
    ISBN 0–8156–2691–6 (cl : alk. paper)—ISBN 0–8156–0332–0
(pb : alk. paper)
    1. Wells, H. G. (Herbert George), 1866–1946—Criticism and
interpretation. 2. Wells, H. G. (Herbert George), 1866–1946.
Time machine. 3. Science fiction, English—History and criticism.
4. Time travel in literature. 5. Prophecies in literature.
6. Future in literature. I. Title. II. Series.
PR5777.P38   1995
823'.912—dc20   95-21827

Manufactured in the United Kingdom

For Jenny

Contents

Preface and Acknowledgments

Poets are the hierophants of an unapprehended inspiration, the mirrors of the gigantic shadows which futurity casts upon the present . . .

P. B. Shelley, 'A Defence of Poetry'

'With a kind of madness growing upon me, I flung myself into futurity.'

The Time Machine

This study of Wells and science fiction centres on *The Time Machine*, which I believe to be one of the Prophetic Books of the late nineteenth century, casting its own shadow over futurity. The theme of time-travelling and the notion of a time machine have never been more popular than they are at the present day. We still live under the spell of Wells's century-old invention.

Rather like the Traveller himself, in *Shadows of the Future* I use *The Time Machine* as my base to explore a literary and cultural landscape in widening circles. In Part I, I consider in successive chapters the idea of literary prophecy (and its opposite, parody) in relation to the science-fiction genre; the continuity and 'life-history' of Wells's prophetic stance throughout his career; the 'possibilities of space and time' and the sense of human dethronement in *The Time Machine* and *The Island of Doctor Moreau*; Wells's theory of history in the scientific romances and his debt (beginning in *The Time Machine*) to Gibbon's *Decline and Fall*; his literary self-definition as a world citizen and his imaginative quest for a new world; and the complex composition of the Wellsian utopia. Part II deals with Wells's influence on two prominent anti-utopians—Yevgeny Zamyatin and George Orwell— and with his legacy to twentieth-century popular scientific thought and to British and American science fiction. One further exploration, of the literal Thames Valley landscape of *The Time Machine* and its use as a setting in other catastrophe fictions, can be found in *Antici-*

pations: Essays on Early Science Fiction and Its Precursors edited by David Seed, a companion volume in the 'SF Texts and Studies' series.

It seems appropriate to offer at the outset three interrelated propositions which distinguish this book to a greater or lesser extent from other critical studies of Wells and his science fiction:

1. Though he is a prolific and very uneven writer whose masterpieces were largely written at the beginning of his career, it is necessary to read Wells extensively as well as intensively in order to understand his best work. The later writings shed light on the earlier. To distinguish between the the productions of the 'artist' and those of the 'journalist', or between the earlier 'imaginative' and the later 'didactic' works (as so many critics have done) has its uses; but it also blunts curiosity and leads in the end to misrepresentation.

2. Because his best work is assumed to be over by 1910, conventional literary and cultural histories of the first half of the twentieth century nearly all underrate Wells's significance. Equally, they overlook the scientific movement of the time, the connections between fictional and non-fictional writing, and the emergence of genre science fiction. *Shadows of the Future* (especially its final chapter) is thus offered as a contribution to an unwritten history of modernity and its cultural discourse.

3. In Wells we have the fullest embodiment of a particular, perhaps unfashionable, conception of the possibilities of twentieth-century writing: that of the writer as prophet. Since his death, literary criticism has largely turned its back on this aspect of his work. Neither the New Criticism nor its successors such as poststructuralism and postmodernism have seen literary prophecy as a suitable object of attention. (F. R. Leavis, who did see it in this way, condemned Wells and Wellsian prophecy out of hand, and hitched his star to a rival prophet.) As for biography, the main question in recent lives of Wells is whether their subject was a true or a false prophet. He lived and wrote under such intense public scrutiny that the current biographical controversies on this score are largely a continuation of arguments begun in his lifetime.

My concern in *Shadows of the Future* is to show how Wells developed and explored the literary potential of prophecy in new ways. As a young writer, he was deeply influenced by Carlyle. He is a missionary writer and teacher like Blake, Shelley, Carlyle, Emerson, Ruskin, Arnold, Morris, Yeats, Shaw, Orwell, D. H. Lawrence,

Aldous Huxley or Doris Lessing. Like many of these, he came from an Evangelical Protestant background and devised a post-Christian gospel of human fulfilment as an encouragement to his hearers lost in the wilderness. But Wells also found the Carlylean mode of social prophecy too Hebraic and too loosely metaphorical for his purposes. He sought to supplement it with the more oracular and Hellenistic notion of prophecy as the literal revelation of future events. Moreover, his gospel was not primarily one of Work, Art, Culture, Socialism, Sex, Self-Liberation or even Science, but of the Future itself and what it could bring. He is closer than the other modern literary prophets to the Shelleyan ideal of the poet as hierophant of an unapprehended inspiration, and to the prophetic world-soul of Shakespeare's Sonnet 104 which dreams obsessively of things to come.

There is always the probability that revelations about the future will be deeply unwelcome. Like Shelley with his view of the poet as a mirror reflecting shadows, Wells knew Plato's parable of the cave and on one occasion (in 'The Country of the Blind') produced his own version of it. As a prophet, he is like Plato's prisoner who stumbles towards the light: he alone understands the real nature of the flickering shadows that his fellow prisoners see on the walls of the cave, but he cannot easily communicate his knowledge to them. There is an element of self-destructiveness involved in taking on this role, as Wells recognised from *The Time Machine* onwards. He did not necessarily expect posterity's understanding or forgiveness. As Plato writes in the *Republic* of his liberated prisoner (I am quoting from Jowett's translation), 'Men would say of him that he had returned from the place above with his eyes ruined; and that it was better not even to think of ascending; and if anyone tried to loose another and lead him up to the light, let them only catch the offender, and they would put him to death'.

Earlier versions of the following chapters first appeared in *Foundation* (Chapter 5), *Science-Fiction Studies* (Chapters 7 and 8), and the *Wellsian* (Chapter 6, and parts of Chapters 3 and 4). Some material in Chapter 2 first appeared in *Europe*. Chapter 6 has also appeared in *The Ends of the Earth*, ed. Simon Gatrell, and Chapter 7 in *H. G. Wells and Modern Science Fiction*, ed. Darko Suvin and Robert M. Philmus. Chapter 9 appears in an earlier form in *Science Fiction: A Critical Guide*, ed. Patrick Parrinder. All these pieces have been specially revised for this volume. I am grateful to the journals concerned for permission to reprint.

It would be impossible to mention all the debts I have incurred in writing and thinking about Wells over many years—happily an unending task, and one I certainly do not feel I have exhausted here. Of the many Wellsian friends I have made since I first began to publish on his work I wish to mention first my colleagues on the H. G. Wells Society executive, notably John Green, John Hammond, Sylvia Hardy, Chris Rolfe, Michael Draper (Michael Sherborne), and the late Peter Hunot and Bob Watkins. Among countless others who have provided inspiration, encouragement and (not least) ideas are Brian Aldiss, Bernard Bergonzi, Maria Teresa Chialant, Robert Crossley, Michael Foot, David Hughes, David Lake, Bernard Loing, Carlo Pagetti, Robert Philmus, Bonnie Kime Scott, David Smith, Brian Stableford, Leon Stover, Darko Suvin, Denise Terrel, the late Jean-Pierre Vernier, and my student Fernando Porta. They are responsible for many of the good things in this book; I wish for their sakes that I could have done it better. I am also grateful to the University of Reading and to my departmental colleagues for supporting my research over the years, to the staff of the Rare Book Room at the University of Illinois, and to my friends in the English Department there. Finally, my heartfelt thanks go to Jenny Bourne Taylor, to whom this book is dedicated, for her love and unstinting support.

Patrick Parrinder
The University of Reading, 1994

Note on texts and editions cited

Wells's literary output is so large and varied that it is important for the reader to bear in mind a sense of its chronological progression. Rather than constantly repeating dates in the text, I have arranged the first section of the Bibliography in the form of a chronology of his principal works for easy reference.

Wells's non-fictional works, which are mostly out of print, are quoted in the (usually first) editions cited in the footnotes. His novels, however, are available in many different—and frequently unsatisfactory—editions. The extension of posthumous copyright within the European Union from 50 to 70 years means that scholars will not be free to produce improved and corrected texts of his novels in his native country for many years to come. The 1924 Atlantic edition, which usually contains the best texts, was limited to 1,670 sets and has never been reprinted. For this reason, I have followed other recent scholars in citing Wells's novels by part, chapter and section rather than page number. In the case of *The Time Machine*, reference is made to the revised section-divisions of the Atlantic text (reproduced in nearly all modern editions) rather than to the chapter-divisions of the 1895 Heinemann text. All quotations from *The Time Machine*, *The Island of Doctor Moreau*, *The War of the Worlds* and *The First Men in the Moon* are from the text as given in the Oxford World's Classics editions (not yet available in the UK for copyright reasons), except where stated. Works of fiction by other writers are quoted in the modern editions cited in the footnotes.

PART I
The Impatient Imagination

CHAPTER ONE
Science Fiction and the 'Shape of Things to Come'

I

Before the rise of modern science fiction, to be the author of a 'chronicle of things before they are done' (*Chronica de futuro scribet*) was a proverbial figure for folly and madness.[1] Christianity, as a revealed religion, had its scriptures—or book of veiled prophecies—and the most that a new prophet could do was to offer subsidiary forecasts invoking the authority of Biblical interpretation. Such prophets would be held in awe by their followers, while others dismissed them with mockery. Today they might be classified as schizophrenics. Others claiming some insight into the future—astrologers, crystal-gazers, fortune-tellers—were confined to the margins of society. All this was in sharp contrast to the classical world, with its time-honoured and widespread belief in the faculties of divination and foretelling.

The secular tale of the future began in the mid-seventeenth century and slowly gathered pace until, with the overnight success of Sir George Chesney's *The Battle of Dorking* (1871), it became a recognised form of commercial fiction. Best-selling novels about the future from Chesney to George Orwell's *Nineteen Eighty-Four* (1948) and Nevil Shute's *On the Beach* (1957) reflect and cash in upon a general foreboding about potential political and military disasters. At the same time, science fiction since H. G. Wells has given birth to the 'future history', with a much broader and grander timescale than is offered by the disaster novel. Typically, future history novels or novel-series are structured around a detailed anticipatory chronology; such claims as they make to prophetic status are surrounded by layers of ambiguity. Olaf Stapledon's *Last and First Men* (1930)—a

---

1 Paul K. Alkon, *Origins of Futuristic Fiction* (Athens and London: University of Georgia Press, 1988), p. 3. The English version of this phrase is used in one of Donne's sermons.

detailed history of post-human civilisation in the next two billion years—is introduced by a Neptunian 'future man' who claims to be its 'true inspirer', speaking through the author's brain.[2] But the introduction is preceded by a preface, signed by Olaf Stapledon, declaring the book to be a romance and a work of fiction (p. 11). According to Stapledon in his preface, seeking to prophesy 'what will as a matter of fact occur' is certainly futile, since fiction about the future is an 'essay in myth creation'. It is 'not science, but art' (pp. 11–12). But we only need to remember Aristotle's distinction between poetry and 'matter of fact' or history in the *Poetics* to suspect that things are not so simple.

Aristotle thought that poetry was more universal and more philosophical than history because it showed, not what had actually occurred, but what probably and necessarily ought to occur. Poetry, in other words, was what Stapledon calls 'myth creation'. Projected into the future, however, the distinction between poetry and matter of fact is suspect because there is, as yet, no matter of fact. Stapledon's preface states his aim of steering a middle course between 'mere history' on the one hand and mere fantasy on the other:

> To romance of the far future . . . is to attempt to see the human race in its cosmic setting, and to mould our hearts to entertain new values.
>
> But if such imaginative construction of possible futures is to be at all potent, our imagination must be strictly disciplined. We must endeavour not to go beyond the bounds of possibility set by the particular state of culture within which we live. (p. 11)

Anyone capable of outlining what must or is likely to happen will gain the reputation of a prophet, at least if the events foretold are spectacular enough—as, in Stapledon's case, they certainly are. Of one of the great religious prophets it has been said that 'Those who believed in Muhammad . . . accepted his prophethood; those who did not called him poet'.[3] There is what Andrew Martin has called a 'secret affinity' between prophecy and imaginative literature,[4]

2 Olaf Stapledon, *Last and First Men* and *Last Men in London* (Harmondsworth: Penguin, 1972), p. 15. Subsequent page references in text.

3 Mohammad Asfour, 'Literary Prophecy', *Abhath Al-Yarmouk: Literature and Linguistics Series* 4:1 (1986), p. 8.

4 Andrew Martin, *The Mask of the Prophet: The Extraordinary Fictions of Jules Verne* (Oxford: Clarendon Press, 1990), p. 209.

and—since its plausibility does not stand or fall by any particular predictions— the myth-making potency that Stapledon intends in *Last and First Men* may be seen as the literary form of prophetic power.

The critic I. A. Richards, in a 1960 lecture on 'The Future of Poetry', had this to say about prophecy:

> Traditionally, and rightly, the prophet trembles. On him lies a double duty: that of actually swaying the future by his words: and that of being a *true* prophet—not a false one. The penalty for being a false prophet, we may recall, is to be stoned to death.[5]

Richards in this deliberately romantic flight is running together two versions of prophecy, the classical image of the trembling priestess or Sibyl and the Hebraic notion of the preacher who may be subject to death by stoning. His remarks are taken from a discussion of poems as the 'unacknowledged legislation of the world' (p. 106)—a claim that with due qualifications can also be made for science fiction.

Richards himself is more widely known as a prophet (usually as an exploded one) in another, perhaps looser, sense. His championship of Basic English, a rationalised and simplified form of the English language, has led, in some quarters, to the intellectual equivalent of stoning. There are in fact certain connections between Richards and H. G. Wells: Richards together with his pupil William Empson was associated with the early twentieth-century 'Scientific Enlightenment' discussed in Chapter Nine below, and he acknowledged Wells's formative influence over his early philosophical notions.[6] The vocation of the 'social prophet' or driven and forward-looking campaigning intellectual took Richards away from his early home in

5 I. A. Richards, 'The Future of Poetry', in *The Screens and Other Poems* (New York: Harcourt, Brace, 1960), p. 105. Subsequent page references in text.

6 In a conversation with me in June 1967 Richards said that the work of Wells which had impressed him most was the pragmatist essay 'Scepticism of the Instrument' (1903). Here Wells argued that the logical categories inherited from Greek thought—number, definition, class and abstract form—were 'regrettable conditions rather than essential facts', conditioned by the imperfections of the human mind as a thinking instrument. Richards later gave to one of his books the title *Speculative Instruments* (1955). See H. G. Wells, *A Modern Utopia* (London: Chapman & Hall, 1905), p. 382.

Cambridge literary criticism just as it took Wells away from the mainstream novel.

What, if any, is the relationship between social prophecy and creative or literary prophecy—between the exhortations of the missionary intellectual and the writing of prophetic fiction? In the seventeenth and eighteenth centuries, early novels about the future had very little in common with the religious prophecies of the time. Paul K. Alkon in *Origins of Futuristic Fiction* sees a radical incompatibility between the two forms of discourse. Religious prophecy, as a form of Biblical interpretation, was allegorical, retrospective and authority-ridden; futuristic fiction was based on irresponsible invention and a 'novelistic piling up of details'. The religious prophet laid claim to truth, the novelist merely to verisimilitude.[7] The nineteenth century fundamentally changed the terms of this discussion, in ways that Alkon, for one, does not address. Thomas Carlyle's essay 'Signs of the Times' (1829) sweeps aside the clamour of millennarian vaticination and announces in its stead the vocation of the social or cultural prophet: to inspect and discern the 'signs of our own time', not of the future.[8] Other Romantic Protestant writers—Wordsworth, Shelley, Matthew Arnold—treat the language of Biblical prophecy as a source of metaphors for the role of the poet or critic. Carlyle in *On Heroes and Hero-Worship* traces a line of spiritual descent from the founders of the great monotheistic religions, Jesus and Mohammed, to the alienated and struggling modern Man of Letters. Admittedly, what was becoming lost in these metaphorical applications of the idea of prophecy was the notion of speaking the truth *about the future*. To write *for* the future, as an 'unacknowledged legislator' or misunderstood genius, is not the same as foretelling it. Nineteenth-century historicism implies, however, that to know the present fully is to know the future, since the one must inexorably follow from the other. Social prophets alert their readers to the present by warning them of that to which the present must lead.

Throughout the twentieth century, social prophecy has played a part in the literature of political protest. The history of opposition to nuclear weapons, for example, includes prophetic writings by such famous intellectuals as Bertrand Russell and E. P. Thompson, who

7 Alkon, *Origins of Futuristic Fiction*, pp. 60–61.
8 Thomas Carlyle, 'Signs of the Times' in *Critical and Miscellaneous Essays* (London: Chapman & Hall, n.d.), II, p. 232.

use future scenarios and draw on science fiction for some of their narrative techniques. A more strictly modern development is the employment of future scenarios by policy-makers and academic experts not concerned with addressing a wider public. (Such scenarios, it is true, have long been in use in such specialised fields as military strategy.) Social and political forecasting has been institutionalised as futurology or 'future studies', a discipline committed to the belief that 'responsible efforts' to see what lies ahead can help us to control our destiny.[9] A contemporary historian and disciple of Wells, W. Warren Wagar, advocates a science of 'hypothetics', aiming to 'pursue various hypotheses about the future in enough technical detail to assess their validity' (p. xv). Yet Wagar presents his outline of twenty-first century history in the form of a future textbook compiled by a fictional character who, like Stapledon's Neptunian narrator, is there to vouch for its 'truth'.

Carlyle's cultural prophecies, too, involved a crucial element of fictional invention—his Professors Teufelsdröckh and Sauerteig. Moreover, they were based on a strong sense of the *Zeitgeist* and epochal change. Carlyle is the theorist of history in the higher sense—transcending Aristotle's idea of history as matter of fact— since for him it is a 'real Prophetic Manuscript' in which the future can be interpreted or guessed at.[10] This brings historicism and futuristic fiction into close contact, a contact observable in Carlyle's own time—in Mary Shelley's novel *The Last Man* (1826), for example—and frequently renewed during the last century and a half of transition from social prophecy to 'future studies'. What distinguishes fictional invention in this area, as often as not, is its knowing ambivalence, its use of distanced and oracular narrative forms and readiness to resort to self-parody. In the introduction to *The Last Man*, Mary Shelley and her husband visit the cave of the Cumæan Sibyl at Baiæ in 1818. Leaves and bark covered with writings in various languages, including English, are strewn about the floor. Among these 'slight Sibylline pages' is (lo and behold!) the subsequent narrative.[11] With Shelley's successor Edgar Allan Poe, we cannot always tell what sort of parody is meant; but there is no ambiguity in

9 W. Warren Wagar, *A Short History of the Future*, 2nd edn. (London: Adamantine Press, 1992), p. xii. Subsequent page references in text.

10 Thomas Carlyle, 'On History' in *Critical and Miscellaneous Essays*, II, pp. 258–59.

11 Mary Shelley, *The Last Man* (London: The Hogarth Press, 1958), p. 3.

his story 'Mellonta Tauta' (1849). The title is a Sophoclean phrase meaning 'These things are in the future', and the very first lines of this letter written on board a balloon on 1 April 2848 announce it as a hoax.

As I. A. Richards reminds us, there is a penalty for being a false prophet. The art of the futuristic novelist is to claim some of the authority of prophecy while avoiding the penalty for being caught out. A false prophet is disproved by events. Wells spoke of the 'self-destructive challenge' involved in fiction about the future;[12] and it is a challenge which some writers prefer to meet more directly than others. Poe's cosmological essay 'Eureka', which of course is a 'Prose Poem' rather than a novel, is marvellously tongue-in-cheek in its truth claims ('I offer this Book of Truths, not in its character of Truth-Teller, but for the Beauty that abounds in its Truth; constituting it true', its author asserts).[13] Olaf Stapledon is one of the straight men of science fiction: wary of laying claim to literal truth, he is also anxious not to be seen as a purveyor of falsehoods. No sooner has he claimed mythic rather than prophetic status for *Last and First Men* than he feels compelled to distinguish between true and false myth:

> A true myth is one which, within the universe of a certain culture . . . , expresses richly, and often perhaps tragically, the highest admirations possible within that culture. A false myth is one which either violently transgresses the limits of credibility set by its own cultural matrix, or expresses admirations less developed than those of its culture's best vision.
> (pp. 11–12)

As author of *Last and First Men*, Stapledon claims to be producing a true myth rather than an undisciplined fantasy. In this way he is doubly defended against the penalty attached to false prophecy.

H. G. Wells in different moods situates himself at varying points along the continuum that separates the playfulness of Poe from Stapledonian truth and seriousness. Wells unlike Stapledon is anxious to have his prophethood recognised, yet his way of being a prophet involves both self-inflation and energetic self-deprecation. No writer has been more given to producing future scenarios than

12 H. G. Wells, 'Utopias', in *Science-Fiction Studies* 27 (July 1982), p. 117. Subsequent page references in text.

13 Edgar Allan Poe, *Eureka*, in *The Science Fiction of Edgar Allan Poe*, ed. Harold Beaver (Harmondsworth: Penguin, 1976), p. 209.

Wells, and his oracular titles such as *The War That Will End War* and *The Shape of Things to Come* have passed into the language and ought to be found in any dictionary of quotations. Nevertheless, he claimed to regret spending so much of his time on this 'ephemeral but amusing' art.[14] 'There is little prospect of any futuristic writings becoming permanent literature', he said in a 1939 talk on 'Utopias': 'We prophets write for our own time and pass almost before we are dead' (p. 117). In a second talk, 'Fiction about the Future', he declared that prophetic writers should aim at the 'illusion of reality', producing the effect of 'an historical novel, the other way round' (p. 247); but this was difficult enough in the novel, and even worse in the cinema where the minutest attention to visual details was necessary. He had never attempted a novel (as opposed to a romance or pseudo-history) set in the future because he could never satisfy himself with the first chapter (p. 249). Recounting the 'detailed improbability' of the culminating scenes of the film he made with Alexander Korda, he ended with this parting shot:

> Suppose one of us or all of us had a real prophetic vision— exact and full of detail—of the buildings, rooms, garments of a hundred years hence—and suppose we had actually put that on the screen, would it have been even as convincing as the stuff we contrived? (p. 250)

Fredric Jameson has argued that contemporary science fiction's deepest vocation is 'to demonstrate and to dramatize our incapacity to imagine the future'; that is, it succeeds by failing.[15] Both Wells and Jameson perceive the ironic condition of prophecy and find in that irony a certain glimmer of hope, though the hope is different in each case. Jameson discovers amid science fiction's pseudo-prophecies the 'impossible and inexpressible Utopian impulse' (p. 157). Wells envisages that would-be prophetic writers might somehow, inadvertently, stumble upon the truth, bringing some authentic 'news from nowhere' to their readers. But then, and only then, they would

14 H. G. Wells, 'Fiction about the Future', in Patrick Parrinder and Robert M. Philmus, eds., *H. G. Wells's Literary Criticism* (Sussex: Harvester Press, and New Jersey: Barnes & Noble, 1980), p. 250. Subsequent page references in text.

15 Fredric Jameson, 'Progress Versus Utopia; or, Can We Imagine the Future?' in *Science-Fiction Studies* 27 (July 1982), p. 153. Subsequent page references in text.

suffer the legendary fate of Cassandra, and be mocked as false prophets.

II

Science fiction is not necessarily or entirely fiction set in the future, but it is closely cognate with it. All observers agree that the presence of an innovation—'the strange property or the strange world', as Wells put it—distinguishes the SF story.[16] According to Darko Suvin, the defining feature of science fiction is the 'narrative dominance or hegemony of a fictional "novum" (novelty, innovation) validated by cognitive logic'.[17] The 'novum' acts to alter the author's empirical environment in determinate ways. This altered environment may be an elsewhere or elsewhen or both, but the more that our knowledge of the global and spatial environment has extended, the greater the pressure on the writer to project the displacement in time. In 1872 Samuel Butler, in *Erewhon*, could legitimately (if satirically) describe a strange world waiting to be discovered 'Over the Range'. Nowadays he would have to invoke space travel. Science fiction depending on new means of transport or scientific discoveries is inevitably set in the future unless the author invokes such artificial devices as a secret invention or an alternative past.

Once we have granted the artist his or her 'novum', Stapledon's ideal of disciplined imagination bounded by possibility has much in common with Suvin's appeal to cognitive logic as a validating principle. Earlier definitions of science fiction speak of the necessity of a 'scientific explanation' to justify the fictional novelty. It may be objected, however, that all such formulations rest on a conception of intellectual responsibility and seriousness that science fiction is not necessarily trying to live up to. Actual science fiction rarely resembles the scenarios put together by futurologists and 'think-tanks', except in very superficial respects. This is because, while the scientific explanation or parade of cognitive logic is one of the genre's conventions, it is also in most cases quite transparently fictive. What the writers are best at is an imitation or parody of logic.

In this respect the artist's apparent role is not that of a prophet but

16 H. G. Wells, 'Preface to *The Scientific Romances*', in Parrinder and Philmus, eds., *H. G. Wells's Literary Criticism*, p. 241. Subsequent page references in text.

17 Darko Suvin, *Positions and Presuppositions in Science Fiction* (Basingstoke: Macmillan, 1988), p. 66.

a magician. H. G. Wells saw his early scientific romances as involving
the displacement of magic by a new, more plausible kind of spell. 'It
occurred to me', he wrote in the 1933 'Preface to The Scientific
Romances', 'that instead of the usual interview with the devil or a
magician, an ingenious use of scientific patter might with advantage
be substituted' (pp. 241–42). The uses of 'scientific patter' are
evident, whether it is the Time Traveller, Dr Moreau, Griffin or
Cavor who does the explaining. It is true that the idea of 'cognitive
logic' goes beyond the justification of new inventions, whether of
invisibility, bio-engineering, or machines for time or space travel, to
the structures of the strange worlds and experiences to which the
invention gives access. Nevertheless, in all Wells's romances the
logical unfolding leads to parodic, ironic reversals. The Time Traveller who goes beyond the period of his own death only to witness the
death of the species, the lunar explorer imprisoned and possibly
killed by the Selenites he so much admires, the Martian invaders
destroyed not by humanity but by terrestrial bacteria—what are
these but illustrations of hubris followed by nemesis, of a logic so
neatly rounded that it speaks of poetic even more than of scientific or
cognitive justice? The existence of fundamental flaws in the logic
underlying Wells's scientific romances has been alleged from time to
time ever since they were first published. For example, Wells himself
pointed out that the Invisible Man must have been blind if his eyes
were invisible.[18] His science-fiction contemporary M. P. Shiel
observed that the Time Traveller ought to have died as he voyaged
into the future and that civilisation on Mars could not have survived
if the bacteria had been eliminated.[19] If cognitive logic were needed
to validate the invention then a great deal would hang on whether or
not we felt that such allegations could be refuted. But in practice they
are a posteriori and marginal to the artistic effect.

The prehistory of science fiction, from Lucian through Swift and
Voltaire to Poe, is full of literary hoaxes and forms of parody. In this
respect SF does not differ from other kinds of fiction aiming at the
illusion of reality. According to the theory of Mikhail Bakhtin,
parody is one of the fundamental devices of the novel and perhaps of

18 H. G. Wells, letter to Arnold Bennett (1897) in Harris Wilson, ed.,
Arnold Bennett and H. G. Wells: A Record of a Personal and a Literary Friendship
(London: Hart-Davis, 1960), pp. 34–35.

19 M. P. Shiel, Science, Life and Literature (London: Willliams & Norgate,
1950), pp. 108–09.

all literature. When we consider Bakhtin's suggestion that 'in world literature there are probably many works whose parodic nature has not even been suspected', then the 'future histories' of SF writers with their meticulous chronologies and impeccable parade of cognitive logic must surely come to mind.[20]   What then is the difference between a story validated by cognitive logic and a story validated by a parody of logic? A parody of logic such as the *reductio ad absurdum* is, after all, a recognised form of logic. Similarly it might be said that a parody of mathematics is a form of mathematics and that a musical pastiche is a form of music. The logician, the mathematician and the musician should all find such paradoxes tolerable. But could scientists accept that there was no fundamental distinction between a scientific explanation and a parody of such an explanation?

It is possible to give examples of scientific theories which began, more or less, in the mode of parody. The Victorian physicist James Clerk-Maxwell is generally held responsible for the notion that a gas consists of invisible molecules bumping into one another like billiard balls. Apparently Clerk-Maxwell could hardly credit this notion when he first advanced it as a speculative hypothesis. Yet it seemed to explain most of the physical and chemical phenomena of gases, so he gradually came to believe in it. The model of a gas as a space full of little invisible bouncy balls came to be universally accepted in science.[21]

I have recounted this example in a deliberately 'unscientific' way, heightening the element of parody. This leads to another point: orthodox science and scientific logic may not be incompatible with parody, but they have little tolerance of it. Once the 'crazy hypothesis' like Clerk-Maxwell's has come to be believed, it is no longer parodic. Logic, by contrast, marginalises parody without eliminating it: the *reductio ad absurdum* has no special or privileged status as a philosophical device. Literature foregrounds the possibility of parody, though whether a parody is actually perceived depends on the reading conventions we bring to the text. Some critics, like Bakhtin and William Empson, see parody everywhere, while others see it virtually nowhere. What is peculiar to science fiction and its

20 M. M. Bakhtin, *The Dialogic Imagination: Four Essays*, ed. Michael Holquist (Austin: University of Texas Press, 1981), p. 374.

21 See Ian Hacking, *Representing and Intervening: Introductory Topics in the Philosophy of Natural Science* (Cambridge: Cambridge University Press, 1983), p. 30.

use of (fictive) cognitive logic as its validating principle is its equal and opposite attraction towards the two poles of prophecy and parody.

III

Parody in the broadest terms is defined by Linda Hutcheon as 'repetition with difference', implying a distance usually signalled by irony between an earlier text and the new one.[22] If parody thus looks backward, the prophetic element in futuristic fiction based on a cognitive innovation or 'novum' is necessarily forward-looking. The notion or hypothesis of the co-presence of prophecy and parody allows us to spell out the conditions according to which the future can be imagined and narrated.

Absolute novelty is not in question, since all that the most startling prophecy can offer is a relative novelty, at least once the prophecy is encoded in language. The worlds of science fiction are not even like the worlds that Alice discovered down the rabbit-hole—nor can the latter be described as prophetic. The demands of possibility and verisimilitude (Stapledon's 'disciplined imagination') ensure that the future can only be modelled on what we already know. The hidden tendencies of the present may be made manifest, its worst fears realised, or a set of entirely comprehensible forces may bring about a world shockingly unlike the one that we now think we inhabit; and in each case our response must be tinged with irony. 'If this goes on', 'That's what it's really like', and 'This is where it's leading to' are characteristic prophetic assertions made by science-fiction texts. The future parodying the present is a favourite trope. (Arguably, the rules of probability and plausibility which produce such parodies are one of the principal reasons why science-fiction writers get the future wrong; but a writer who warns against a future that fails to materialise may, as we saw above, lay claim to the mantle of cultural prophecy.)

The co-presence of prophecy and parody (that is, of genuine novelty and repetition with difference) is often apparent from the opening sentences of works in which the future setting is presented as an immediate given, without the need for the narrator to travel or for the reader to be transported there. The beginning of George Orwell's *Nineteen Eighty-Four* is a famous example:

22 Linda Hutcheon, *A Theory of Parody: The Teachings of Twentieth-Century Art Forms* (New York and London: Methuen, 1985), p. 32.

> It was a bright cold day in April, and the clocks were striking
> thirteen.

Nasty, British and short (the continental 24-hour clock being seen as
an affront to English insularity), this tells us that we are in for a
gloomy, technologically backward dystopia. The parody of traditional narratives setting out in springtime instantly conveys the loss of
hope.

Orwell writes as a deliberate satirist. Science fiction more typically
tends to routinise prophecy and parody in opening sentences or
paragraphs that eschew flamboyance and seem anxious not to call
attention to themselves. How many readers, for example, have
paused over the Time Traveller's chairs which, 'being his patents,
embraced and caressed us rather than submitted to be sat upon'
(§1)? What more appropriate setting could there be for a discourse
on 'recondite matters' in which the Traveller will invite his guests to
discard some of their most elementary philosophical preconceptions? The guests, having submitted to the embrace of a new form of
chair, are like hypnotic subjects, open to suggestion. Without firmer
and more rigid back-support they are presumably lost from the start?
The opening of *The War of the Worlds* is much more melodramatic:

> No one would have believed in the last years of the nine-
> teenth century that this world was being watched keenly
> and closely by intelligences greater than man's and yet as
> mortal as his own; that as men busied themselves about their
> various concerns they were scrutinised and studied, perhaps
> almost as narrowly as a man with a microscope might
> scrutinise the transient creatures that swarm and multiply in
> a drop of water. (I,1)

Here we are seized with the idea of a logical reversal, with other
intelligences looking at us in the same way as a 'man with a
microscope' would scrutinise biological specimens; but the early part
of the sentence is also quietly devastating in its way. No-one would
have believed this in the last years of the nineteenth century;
everyone (the narrator implies) believes it 'now'. In sentences like
these, the future is a mental and physical landscape to which we
must acclimatise, but it is also a kind of joke. We are simultaneously
drawn into it and held at a distance. The future by definition must be
different, but difference can always be understood in terms of
grotesque repetition. Sentences like these establish what Bakhtin

would call the double-voiced narration of the science-fiction text, as a discourse poised between prophecy and parody.

IV

Opening sentences are 'indexes' (as Nestor says in Shakespeare's *Troilus and Cressida*) in which there is seen

> The baby figure of the giant mass
> Of things to come at large. (I.3.343–46)

A writer who intends to engage explicitly and categorically with notions of prophecy will lose no time in moving from the baby figure to the giant mass. Wells in *The Time Machine* begins with a miniature model of the Time Traveller's invention, which the Psychologist sends hurtling into the future with a flick of his finger. Later, the Time Traveller himself pauses in his journey only to find the threshold of the future guarded by a colossal statue, that of the White Sphinx. This brooding prophetic symbol has a number of sources, among them Jules Verne's novel *Le Sphinx des glaces* (a sequel to Poe's *Narrative of Arthur Gordon Pym*) and the ring of great statues forming 'a sort of Stonehenge', 'worn and lichen-grown', that Samuel Butler's narrator discerns through a veil of cloud as he reaches the top of the range and prepares to descend into Erewhon.[23] Butler's hero faints in front of the statues, while the Time Traveller, who sees the Sphinx at first indistinctly through a cloud of hail, falls into a kind of hypnotic trance: ' "I stood looking at it for a little space—half a minute, perhaps, or half an hour" '(§3). In each case the confrontation inspires a series of questions:

> What, then, was to be my fate at the hands of its inhabitants? Should I be taken and offered up as a burnt-offering to those hideous guardians of the pass? (*Erewhon*, p. 50)

> 'What might appear when that hazy curtain was altogether withdrawn? What might not have happened to men? What if cruelty had grown into a common passion? What if in this interval the race had lost its manliness, and had developed into something inhuman, unsympathetic, and overwhelmingly powerful?' (*The Time Machine*, §3)

23 Samuel Butler, *Erewhon, or Over the Range* (London: Cape, 1932), p. 48. Subsequent page references in text.

' "I looked up again at the crouching white shape" ', says Wells's narrator (§3); and it was the word 'shape', recalling Shelley's prophetic 'Shadows' and 'Shapes' and Coleridge's 'shaping spirit' of imagination, that Wells would later add to the Shakespearean phrase 'things to come'.

'Shape' here has two meanings. It is at once a question of shaping the future in a plastic or narrative sense, and of perceiving the future with awe and foreboding as a shape already given. The one is the task of the narrators or storytellers of futuristic fiction, while the other is the experience or revelation they have to impart. Both Wells and Butler prefigure that experience through their dimly seen statues that prompt the traveller to ask his prophetic questions. The questions will, inevitably, be answered. As Mohammad Asfour has stated, prophecy in literature is a narrative device creating a sense of expectation that has to be fulfilled if it is to be functional at all.[24] In *The Time Machine* the prophetic symbol within the text functions as a kind of initiation ritual, joining the as yet unknown future to the prehistoric past out of which the Sphinx comes. The existence of a future Sphinx is a grotesque repetition implying that what is to come is (like the Sphinx's famous riddle, to which the answer is 'a man') no more and no less than what we already know.

Butler's narrator's fear of being sacrificed as a burnt-offering, and the Time Traveller's foreboding of a race that has 'lost its manliness', are universal anxieties cast in inescapably nineteenth-century terms. Such prophecies may or may not have been read as parodies at the time; in retrospect they certainly can be. Yet this does not diminish these works as Wells thought it would. Their questions repeat, and also innovate upon, the unanswered question 'Then, what is life?' which resounds so despairingly at the end of Shelley's unfinished poem 'The Triumph of Life'. The argument against literal prophecy—that, even if foreknowledge exists, it is better to live in ignorance of impending misfortunes—has often been put, and by none more eloquently than Cicero in his diatribe against the classical oracles.[25] The Time Traveller may have appreciated this point as he stood before the Sphinx. Science fiction, however, relies upon our hunger for foreknowledge and our need to contemplate shadows of

24 Mohammad Asfour, 'Literary Prophecy', p. 16.
25 Marcus Tullius Cicero, *On Divination*, in *Brutus, On the Nature of the Gods, On Divination, On Duties*, trans. Hubert M. Poteat (Chicago: University of Chicago Press, 1950), pp. 404–05.

the future as part of the process of self-discovery. Wells, like many of his successors in the genre, was a scientific materialist who believed that the nature of life would only be unfolded within a temporal (or, at best, spatial-temporal) perspective. This meant that the duty of prophecy was laid upon any writer who set out to answer Shelley's question.

CHAPTER TWO
The Broken Tripod and the Impatient Imagination

I

H. G. Wells has not one but several kinds of reputation as a prophet. He foresaw future wars and anticipated the weapons of war, notably the aeroplane, the tank and the atomic bomb.[1] He was a tireless campaigner for a new form of political organisation, the world state, to which the adjective 'Wellsian' has frequently been attached. In the age of the bicycle he spoke of the prospects of genetic engineering and space travel. He used future settings in many works of fiction, speculating sometimes on immediate possibilities and sometimes on the ultimate destiny of the human species and its planet. In his last book *Mind at the End of Its Tether* he took stock of his whole career and wrote as follows: 'The habitual interest of [the writer's] life is critical anticipation. Of everything he asks: "To what will this lead?" '[2] John Middleton Murry in an obituary notice described him as the 'last prophet of bourgeois Europe',[3] though he was also perhaps its first futurologist.

Wells greeted the twentieth century with a book of extrapolative essays called *Anticipations of the Reaction of Mechanical and Scientific Progress upon Human Life and Thought*. Five years later, he introduced a travel book significantly entitled *The Future in America* with a chapter analysing 'The Prophetic Habit of Mind'. In *The Discovery of the Future*, a discourse given at the Royal Institution in 1902, he argued that scientific prediction was both useful and possible. Many of his non-fiction titles proclaim their concern with futurology and critical anticipation. These include *The War that Will End War*, *What Is*

1 In *When the Sleeper Wakes*, 'The Land Ironclads' and *The World Set Free* respectively.

.2 H. G. Wells, *Mind at the End of Its Tether* (London: Heinemann, 1945), pp. 4–5. Subsequent page references in text.

3 Reprinted in Patrick Parrinder, ed., *H. G. Wells: The Critical Heritage* (London and Boston: Routledge & Kegan Paul, 1972), p. 347.

Coming?, War and the Future, A Year of Prophesying, A Forecast of the World's Affairs, The Way the World Is Going, The Fate of Homo Sapiens and *The Happy Turning*. The later Wells made anticipation his trademark, while the early Wells mixed prophecy with playful self-parody.

Prophecy and parody are intermingled in the apprentice writings that he produced as a science student in the 1880s. These included 'A Vision of the Past' (a story of time-travel to the age of the dinosaurs) and 'A Tale of the Twentieth Century (for Advanced Thinkers)'. In 1888, a few months after the disastrous footballing accident that terminated his career as a resident schoolmaster, he wrote to his friend A. Morley Davies that 'I have coughed up recently a lot more gorey [?] lung, so I am afraid the hungry maw will presently engulph the Prophet of the Undelivered Spell, and the unwarned world hurry on to damnation'.[4] Wells at this point was an avid reader of Carlyle; but he sought to supplement the latter's Hebraic and Biblical cast of mind with a more Hellenistic and oracular notion of prophecy as the literal revelation of future events. In the same year as the letter to Davies he published 'The Chronic Argonauts', the earliest version of *The Time Machine*, and wrote to another friend, Elizabeth Healey, that it was 'no joke. There is a sequel—It is the latest Delphic voice but the Tripod is not yet broken'.[5]

The Delphic tripod was a simple cooking utensil, suitable perhaps for burnt offerings or incense. A metal plate or lid fitted to the bowl of the tripod enabled it to be used as a seat.[6] The priestess or Pythia, an ordinary peasant woman more than fifty years old, possessed no special powers when not seated upon the tripod.[7] According to one version, the seat was a safety device to prevent the trembling prophetess from falling into the chasm beneath her cell. However, there is no reference to the tripod being literally broken, and even in the legendary struggle for its possession between Apollo and Herakles it survived intact. Wells doubtless grasps at the metaphor of breaking in his letter to Healey because—as in the earlier letter to

4 MS. Wells Collection, University of Illinois.

5 MS. Wells Collection, University of Illinois. Quoted in Bernard Loing, *H. G. Wells à l'oeuvre: Les débuts d'un écrivain (1894–1900)* (Paris: Didier, 1984), p. 406.

6 Robert Flacelière, *Greek Oracles*, trans. D. Garman (London: Elek, 1965), p. 44.

7 H. W. Parke, *Greek Oracles* (London: Hutchinson, 1967). p. 73.

Davies—he has in mind the breaking of a spell, which allows it to be 'delivered' or put into words. The prophetess in the act of divination is spellbound, and receives her vision; the words that fall from her are indicative of the vision, but she cannot articulate or 'spell it out'. Spelling out and recording the oracle in hexameters was the task of the *Prophetes*, the Pythia's learned and priestly attendant.[8] Spelling, as in the verb 'to spell', thus implies both a state of enchantment or incantation and the writing down of the inspired message after the spell is broken. A speaker in Plutarch's dialogue 'On the Pythian Oracles' argues that all that the god does is to inspire the Pythia with a general vision of the truth and the future. The actual words in which the vision is transmitted are ordinary human language chosen either by her or by the priests.[9] A similarly double process of inspiration and articulation is implied by one of the most influential Romantic accounts of the creative process, Shelley's 'Defence of Poetry'. For Shelley, poets are 'hierophants of an unapprehended inspiration'.[10] The young Wells, too, projected himself in these terms.

Despite his assertion that 'The Chronic Argonauts' was no joke, his apprentice pieces are the products of a writer with the desire to be a prophet but without, as yet, any startling truths to reveal. 'A Tale of the Twentieth Century' is mildly satirical, using the theme of perpetual motion which he had already exploited as a practical joke to amuse his friends in the college Debating Society.[11] 'The Chronic Argonauts', partly a pastiche of Hawthorne,[12] has the form but not the content of a prophetic tale. In it, Wells outlines the idea of a time machine—an idea somehow analogous to that of perpetual motion—but makes no attempt to take his readers into the future.

The Time Machine, with its brooding symbol of the sphinx, is the 'sequel' to 'The Chronic Argonauts' and Wells's first authentically prophetic tale. The earliest surviving version of the Time Traveller's encounter with the sphinx appeared under the title 'A.D. 12,203: A

8 Ibid., p. 84.

9 Robert Flacelière, *Greek Oracles*, p. 84.

10 Percy Bysshe Shelley, 'A Defence of Poetry', in *Shelley's Prose in the Bodleian Manuscripts*, ed. A. H. Koszul (London: Frowde, 1910), p. 117.

11 See Geoffrey West, *H. G. Wells: A Sketch for a Portrait* (London: Howe, 1930), p. 61.

12 See Bernard Bergonzi, *The Early H. G. Wells* (Manchester: Manchester University Press, 1961), pp. 30–31.

Glimpse of the Future' in W. E. Henley's *National Observer* in 1894; but this was preceded by an openly parodic account of the future of the human species, 'The Man of the Year Million', published in the *Pall Mall Gazette* in November 1893. Here Wells offers a Carlylean précis of a learned tome called 'The Necessary Character of the Man of the Remote Future deduced from the Existing Stream of Tendency', by one Professor Holzkopf, 'presumably Professor at Weissnichtwo'.[13] Ostensibly, this fantasy (which Wells later drew upon for the structure of the Martians in *The War of the Worlds*) is a work of academic futurology; but the fictitious professor evidently shares his author's capacity for a kind of visionary rhetoric giving to the 'coming man' a form and shape:

> 'There grows upon the impatient imagination a building, a dome of crystal, across the translucent surface of which flushes of the most glorious and pure prismatic colours pass and fade and change. In the centre of this transparent chameleon-tinted dome is a circular white marble basin filled with some clear, mobile, amber liquid, and in this plunge and float strange beings. Are they birds?
>
> 'They are the descendants of man—at dinner.' (p. 112)

The crystal dome with transient colours flashing across its surface is at once a future building and a self-reflexive prophetic image, anticipating Wells's later short story 'The Crystal Egg' and referring to the fortune-teller's crystal ball. The crystal dome and what it contains become apparent to the 'impatient imagination'.

Many years afterwards, in a passage explaining the creative genesis of his early short stories, Wells again implicitly likened the imagination to a crystal ball:

> I found that, taking almost anything as a starting-point and letting my thoughts play about it, there would presently come out of the darkness, in a manner quite inexplicable, some absurd or vivid little incident . . . . Little men in canoes upon sunlit oceans would come floating out of nothingness, incubating the eggs of prehistoric monsters unawares; violent conflicts would break out amidst the flower-beds of suburban gardens; I would discover I was peering into

---

13 H. G. Wells, 'Of a Book Unwritten' in *Certain Personal Matters* (London: Unwin, 1901), p. 108. Subsequent page references in text.

remote and mysterious worlds ruled by an order logical indeed but other than our common sanity.[14]

In Wellsian terms, the image of peering into remote and mysterious worlds carries suggestions both of scientific observation through the lens of a telescope or microscope, and of the visionary discoveries made by the 'impatient imagination'. The resulting narratives, to adapt T. S. Eliot's words describing the creative process, just ' "came" '.[15] We can sum up the young Wells as a writer hungry for inspiration whose imaginative impatience was—necessarily—turned towards the future.

II

In Wells the Hebraic notion of the preacher and sage—a literary Moses pointing the way to his own version of the Promised Land and warning of dire consequences if his message is unheeded—is overlaid with the classical images of the Delphic priestess, sphinx and Sibyl. Perhaps the archetypal classical prophet is Cassandra, the messenger of doom whose fate it is that nobody will listen to her. Accordingly, 'The Man of the Year Million' ends with Professor Holzkopf's vison of doom. The earth is cooling and, in search of warmth, the last men are forced underground, ' "in galleries and laboratories deep down in the bowels of the earth" ':

> The whole world will be snow-covered and piled with ice; all animals, all vegetation vanished, except this last branch of the tree of life. The last men have gone even deeper, following the diminishing heat of the planet, and vast metallic shafts and ventilators make way for the air they need. (p. 113)

In this alternative version of the world of the Morlocks, the 'last men' are shown as digging their own graves, deeper and deeper. The only other recourse, taken by the Martians, was to escape into space in the attempt to colonise warmer worlds.

Wells's later future history novels usually take the form of 'dream books', with an outer narrative framing the words of an eye-witness

14 H. G. Wells, 'Introduction' to *The Country of the Blind and Other Stories* (London: Nelson, n.d. [1911], p. iv. Subsequent page references in text.

15 T. S. Eliot, 'Tradition and the Individual Talent' in *The Sacred Wood: Essays on Poetry and Criticism* (London: Methuen, 1960), p. 155.

character and giving them a displaced, oracular quality. The protagonist of *In the Days of the Comet* is first seen as 'the man who wrote in the tower', presumably alluding to the Platonist of Milton's 'Il Penseroso'. Elsewhere, the use of literary allusion and the citation of an 'unwritten literature' is quite explicit. Much of *The World Set Free* consists of a summary of a popular autobiographical Bildungsroman, Frederick Barnet's *Wander Jahre* (1970). *The Shape of Things to Come* is introduced as the 'Dream Book of Dr Philip Raven', and what Raven sees is a 'modern Sibylline book'.[16] The Sibylline history was a convenient cloak for Wells's need to switch back and forth between the roles of Moses and Cassandra.

In Book VI of Virgil's *Aeneid*, the Cumæan Sibyl, 'wrapping truth in darkness', prophesies future wars and the Tiber foaming with streams of blood. Virtually every Wellsian future history is a prophecy of war, beginning with *The War of the Worlds* where not only are the invaders literally bloodthirsty but the Thames turns red due to the growth of the Martian red weed. Towards the end of the novel the narrator wanders deliriously through dead London streets singing 'some inane doggerel about "The Last Man Left Alive!" ' (II, 9). His predecessor is Mary Shelley's Last Man, whose story was supposedly discovered in the Sibyl's cave at Cumae. Other Gothic novels such as Maturin's *Melmoth the Wanderer* and Lewis's *The Monk* also have 'Sibylline' beginnings. The original Sibylline books were a collection of oracular utterances, said to have been sold to Tarquin by the Cumæan Sibyl, which were preserved in ancient Rome and consulted by the Senate in times of emergency. A 'modern Sibylline book' is, therefore, a prophecy of catastrophe which, if properly heeded by the authorities, could lead to the state's salvation.

In his self-appointed role as modern Sibyl, Wells travelled the world in order to have high-profile conversations with Lenin, Stalin, and Theodore and Franklin Roosevelt. The fact that he sought to guide these statesmen rather than challenging the basis of their power may be related to his partial rejection of patriarchal Hebrew images of prophecy in favour of the female symbolism of the classical oracles. *Tono-Bungay* is a prophetic social novel in which the male narrator's impatient imagination struggles to discern the outlines of the new England that is replacing the old one, the 'England of our children's children' (I,1,iii). He compares his task to watching the

16 H. G. Wells, *The Shape of Things to Come: The Ultimate Revolution* (London: Hutchinson, 1933), p. 14.

kind of lantern show which used to be known as the 'Dissolving Views'—a variant on the crystal-gazing image. Eventually, he is driven to protest his devotion to scientific truth, 'the remotest of mistresses' (III,3,i). The Wellsian intellectual protagonist, a male inspired by a female muse, can thus be contrasted with the Sibylline author or Delphic priestess whose female voice is traditionally inspired by a male god. The androgynous sphinx in *The Time Machine* suggests a possible reconciliation of these conflicting intimations of the gendered nature of prophecy. What the sphinx reveals to the Time Traveller is a human race that has grown 'unsympathetic, and overwhelmingly powerful', before losing its 'manliness' (§3).

After *The Time Machine*, Wells produced the remainder of his early scientific romances—*The Island of Doctor Moreau*, *The Invisible Man*, *The War of the Worlds* and *The First Men in the Moon*—and the bulk of his short stories with astonishing swiftness. The intensity of this phase of his writing, and the fact that he left it behind for quite different concerns, are the surest signs of literary genius. They also prompt further questions about the 'impatience' of his prophetic imagination. 'Consumption' was diagnosed after his footballing accident in 1887 and, like other consumptive writers before and after him, he was impelled to write with such speed not merely because he needed the money but because he thought he had little time. In 1897, after ten years on the danger list, he reported in a remarkable brief essay, 'How I Died', that he was still a 'Doomed Man'. Death, he had thought when he was 'full of the vast ambition of youth', was 'quite out of sight', and life was 'still an interminable vista of years'; but then suddenly he 'saw [Death's] face near to my own'.[17] Similarly, the professor in 'The Man of the Year Million' pronounces that 'every man who does think of these things must look eternity in the face' (p. 113); and that is what the Time Traveller does when, having travelled so far beyond the natural period of his own life, he finds the sphinx watching him with its 'sightless eyes' (§3).

Before his journey, we are told, the Time Traveller 'thought but cheerlessly of the Advancement of Mankind, and saw in the growing pile of civilization only a foolish heaping that must inevitably fall back upon and destroy its makers in the end' (Epilogue). That foreboding was, if anything, a spur to him to travel forward and see for himself. But, having learnt of our ultimate destiny, what can we

17 H. G. Wells, 'How I Died', in *Certain Personal Matters*, p. 182. Subsequent page references in text.

do but avert our eyes?—or, as the narrator says of the Time Traveller's vision, 'If that is so, it remains for us to live as though it were not so'. To the narrator, the future remains a 'vast ignorance', it is 'still black and blank' (Epilogue). The Traveller's revelation and the narrator's response may be seen to embody two equal and opposite aspects of prophetic 'impatience'. The first is the prophet's need to know and to relate the worst that can be told—the Doomed Man's urge to confront the ultimate doom of man—and his or her impatience with the world's complacent ignorance. The second, born of the prophet's compassion for humanity at large, is the need to distract them from a hopeless and seemingly pointless knowledge of destiny. What use is it to us to know that everything we can possibly set store by will one day disappear? So the oracular message is veiled; and where there is the least chance of salvation the Hebraic prophet turns from warnings to exhortations. So it was, apparently, with Wells, and as his health improved after 1900 the tone of his books began to change from resigned pessimism to an irascible, hectoring optimism.

III

In the first chapter of *The Future in America*, Wells presents himself not as a Doomed Man but as one who is 'doomed to the prophetic habit of mind':[18]

> This habit of mind confronts and perplexes my sense of things that simply *are*, with my brooding preoccupation with how they will shape presently, what they will lead to, what seed they will sow, and how they will wear. . . . There are days, indeed, when it makes life seem so transparent and flimsy, seem so dissolving, so passing on to an equally transitory series of consequences, that the enhanced sense of instability becomes restlessness and distress; but on the other hand nothing that exists, nothing whatever, remains altogether vulgar or dull or dead or hopeless in its light. But the interest is shifted. (pp. 6–7)

Wells's sense of the flimsiness of things is expressed in the 'Dissolving Views' metaphor of *Tono-Bungay* and also in his comparison of the receding New York skyline, as seen at the end of *The Future in*

18 H. G. Wells, *The Future in America: A Search after Realities* (London: Chapman & Hall, 1906), p. 11. Subsequent page references in text.

America, to 'piled-up packing cases outside a warehouse' (p. 358). We may remember also the descriptions of the experience of time-travelling in *The Time Machine*, and the passage in 'How I Died' in which he recounts the shocking onset of his illness: 'suddenly, with a gout of blood upon my knuckle, with a queer familiar taste in my mouth, . . . this world that had been so solid grew faint and thin' (p. 182).

In *The Future in America* and subsequent works, he finds a philosophical underpinning for his sense of transitoriness in Heraclitus's dictum that ' "There is no Being but Becoming" ' (p. 5). The answer to the question 'What are we to do with our lives?' (used as the title of one of his later books) is that success is to be measured by the individual contribution we are able to make to the general development of human potential. The genetically unique human individual should be understood as an experiment conducted by the species and capable of seeding the future. This belief, first outlined in 'The Rediscovery of the Unique' as early as 1891, links Wells's post-Darwinian biological training to his prophetic concerns; moreover, it sanctions his philosophical affiliations to pragmatism—as announced in his paper 'Scepticism of the Instrument' in 1903—and later to nominalism. It also has quasi-religious undertones which appear in some of his writing, beginning with *First and Last Things*, his 'Confession of Faith and Rule of Life', first published in 1908 and three times subsequently revised. *First and Last Things* sets out his conviction that 'We are episodes in an experience greater than ourselves'.[19] For Wells, to seek knowledge of that greater whole means, essentially, to look forward to the epoch of 'Collective Mind' when what is now largely unconscious will have become conscious.

In *The Future in America* he outlines five stages in the 'life history' of his prophetic mind, showing how his habit of critical anticipation grew out of the orthodox Christian millennialism of his childhood. With Armageddon and the Last Judgment imminent, speculation about the future was at first a 'monstrous joke' (p. 9). Then, as a student of biology, he found his apocalyptic faith disappearing, to be replaced by a 'blackness and a vagueness about the endless vista of years ahead, that was tremendous—that terrified' (p. 10). His response, he now claimed, had been to fill up the emptiness with a 'sudden apprehension of unlimited possibility':

19 H. G. Wells, *First and Last Things: A Confession of Faith and Rule of Life* (London: Watts, 1929), p. 65.

> One made fantastic exaggerations, fantastic inversions of all
> recognized things. . . . The books about the future that
> followed the first stimulus of the world's realization of the
> implications of Darwinian science, have all something of the
> monstrous experimental imaginings of children. I myself, in
> my microcosmic way, duplicated my times. (pp. 10–11)

'The Man of the Year Million' and *The Time Machine* were, he says, books of this sort, and they led to a dead end. But in the third phase he decided to attempt 'something a little more proximate than the final destiny of man' (p. 11).

Wells's dismissal of the 'monstrous' imaginings of the scientific romances reflects his desire, in 1906, to establish his credentials as a serious sociological essayist. Surprisingly, since the five phases of his prophetic development followed so quickly upon one another, he sets out to dismiss each outmoded phase as a form of false prophecy. (Such an onslaught on false prophecy is part of the rhetorical armoury of nearly every prophet, as was hinted in the preceding chapter.) The third and fourth phases of his mental 'life history', in which he began to attempt scientific forecasting—to turn prophecy into futurology—are also brusquely dismissed. The reason given for this is his discovery of the 'inseparable nature of the two functions of the prophet', those of anticipation and exhortation (p. 15).

In the third phase, around 1898–99, Wells turned to the extrapolation of future societies from existing social and technological trends. *When the Sleeper Wakes* and 'A Story of the Days to Come' start out from the overcrowded city of the present day in order to construct a hermetically-sealed twenty-first century megalopolis; but the results were once again more fantastic than plausible, 'a sort of gigantesque caricature of the existing world, everything swollen to vast proportions and massive beyond measure'—or so he now thought (p. 12). The fourth, more genuinely scientific phase of his 'attack upon the future' involved making adjustments for conflicting trends: 'One attempts a rude, wide analysis of contemporary history, one seeks to clear and detach operating causes and to work them out, and so, combining this necessary set of consequences with that, to achieve a synthetic forecast in terms just as broad and general and vague as the causes considered are few' (pp. 12–13). Once again, this may sound impressionistic rather than strictly scientific, but it is the approach taken by innumerable twentieth-century futurological works, beginning with Wells's *Anticipations*. He defended the method more rigorously in The Discovery of the Future, arguing that, just as geologists and archaeologists had recently opened up a new, 'inductive' past, so there might be inductive knowledge of the future. Scientific thought, he maintained, was inherently predictive, since it was by means of the inferences they entailed for future events that scientific theories were usually tested. The scientific discovery of the future had begun with such dramatic examples of prediction as the astronomical calculation of the periodic return of Halley's Comet.

The possibilities and limitations of significant knowledge of the future were determined, Wells suggested in The Discovery of the Future, by something like the 'actuarial principle' used by insurance companies in fixing their premiums. Though individual outcomes remained unknowable, certain sorts of average outcome could be foreseen with a fair degree of certainty. Such methods, Wells conceded in The Future in America, 'really [did] affect a sort of prophecy on the material side of life' (p. 13). But he now claimed to distrust them.

In fact, the momentum of his argument in The Discovery of the Future had taken him beyond a defence of scientific forecasting based on the actuarial principle to the assertion that human development was following a 'rising curve' within the framework of universal evolution.[20] Moreover, in a famously uplifting conclusion he spoke of the 'greatness of human destiny' (p. 34) and imagined that mankind would reach out to the stars. The fifth phase of prophecy in The Future in America rationalises this breaking of the strict confines of scientific futurology. In The Discovery of the Future he had alleged that the 'Great Men' theory of history was overrated; in the later book, however, he perceives an 'incalculable opposition' to mechanical forces in human custom and in the 'poetic power' of exceptional individuals (p. 15). He now claims to be adding Schopenhauerian Will to the bleak picture of Darwinian Necessity: 'Much may be foretold as certain, much more as possible, but the last decisions and the greatest decisions, lie in the hearts and wills of unique incalculable men' (p. 16). So he goes to America, not to 'work a pretentious horoscope' but to find out a 'great nation's Will' and the destiny to which it points (p. 17). Moreover, the prophet's

20 H. G. Wells, The Discovery of the Future with The Common-Sense of World Peace and The Human Adventure, ed. Patrick Parrinder (London: PNL Press, 1989), p. 35. Subsequent page references in text.

own exhortations affect the future he has to investigate, which is why the twin functions of the prophet are inseparable.

Wells in the early years of the century can be seen to vacillate between the attempt to discover meaning and purpose in the evolutionary process (which, broadly speaking, is his position in *The Discovery of the Future*), and an outlook derived from his mentor T. H. Huxley in which human development is seen as an artificial process opposing the natural course of evolution at very point.[21] Significantly, his argument in *The Discovery of the Future* changes direction immediately after a passage reviewing the various kinds of natural catastrophe which might threaten life on earth. Collision with an asteroid, the spread of a new epidemic, the poisoning of the atmosphere by cometary vapours, the emergence of a new species of predator, or self-destruction as a result of collective psychosis are all possible. Added to these is the 'reasonable certainty' of eventual extinction as a result of planetary cooling (p. 34).[22] As at the end of *The Time Machine*, it is when contemplating the message of scientific prophecy at its starkest that he tends to seek refuge in humanist exhortation. So he switches from Cassandra's impatience with human short-sightedness to Moses' impatience to lead mankind away from its bondage to natural contingency.

These twin aspects of Wellsian prophecy were to be graphically captured in his violent mood-swings at the time of the First and Second World Wars—wars whose possibility he had long foreseen. He reacted to the outbreak of hostilities in August 1914 by writing *The War that Will End War*, but a year later this was succeeded by *Boon* with its cynical 'Story of the Last Trump', in which the apocalyptic trumpet sounds by accident on earth but passes unnoticed. Towards the end of the war he dedicated himself to the humanist objective of world education through encyclopaedic textbooks, writing in the first and most influential of these, *The Outline of History*, that human life was becoming 'more and more a race between education and

21 Compare Leon Stover, 'Applied Natural History: Wells vs. Huxley', in Patrick Parrinder and Christopher Rolfe, eds., *H.G.Wells Under Revision: Proceedings of the International H. G. Wells Symposium*, London, July 1986 (Selinsgrove: Susquehanna University Press, and London and Toronto: Associated University Presses, 1990), pp. 125–33.

22 Wells later qualified this in a footnote to the 1913 edition of *The Discovery of the Future* acknowledging that 'the discovery of radio-activity has changed all that' (p. 37).

catastrophe'.[23] Wells very characteristically ended the *Outline* with a section devoted to 'The Next Stage in History'.

In the darkest days of the Second World War, he still thought that education was capable of winning its race with catastrophe. George Orwell accused him in 'Wells, Hitler and the World State' (1941) of being temperamentally incapable of appreciating the full gravity of the totalitarian threat. A year later, Wells wrote that the war, though hideous, was not in itself of the nature of a biological cataclysm, and the birth of the 'After-Man, our bodily and mental offspring, of whom this present time is the Advent' was still attainable by an exercise of human will.[24] It was this faith which failed him when in 1945, in his seventy-ninth year, he came to the unforeseen final phase of his career as a prophet. The opening chapters of *Mind at the End of Its Tether* are a repudiation of all the earlier premises of Wellsian forecasting. Chapter Three is headed, simply, 'There is no "Pattern of Things to Come" '. Here Wells is obsessed by the intuition of a 'harsh queerness' (p. 8) in the 'secular process' or 'cosmic movement' of natural events, resulting in a cosmos that is no longer hospitable to human life. The agency which he calls 'the Antagonist' is about to accomplish the final destruction of mankind. (The only 'evidence' Wells cites is that of the freakish nature of the terrestrial environment in which life began, and the limit set to velocity by the speed of light.) Cassandra-like, he 'puts forward his conclusions in the certainty that they will be entirely inacceptable to the ordinary rational man' (p. 1), and once again he denounces his earlier self as a false prophet:

> it was natural for him to assume that there was a limit set to change, that new things and events would appear, but that they would appear consistently, preserving the natural sequence of life. So that in the present vast confusion of our world, there was always the assumption of an ultimate restoration of rationality, ... It was merely a question, the fascinating question, of what forms the new rational phase would assume, ... To this, the writer set his mind.
>
> He did his utmost to pursue the trends, that upward spiral,

23 H. G. Wells, *The Outline of History: Being a Plain History of Life and Mankind* (London: Cassell, 1920), p. 608. Subsequent page references in text.

24 H. G. Wells, *The Conquest of Time* (London: Watts, 1942), p. 57.

> towards their convergence in a new phase in the story of life, and the more he weighed the realities before him the less was he able to detect any convergence whatever. . . . Hitherto events had been held together by a certain logical consistency, as the heavenly bodies as we know them have been held together by the pull, the golden cord, of Gravitation. Now it is as if that cord had vanished and everything was driving anyhow to anywhere at a steadily increasing velocity. (p. 5)

There is an awesome quality about the cold impersonality of *Mind at the End of Its Tether*, the extent of its repudiations, its blankness of feeling. This shocking final book is at once a reflection of intellectual confusion (Wells was terminally ill when he wrote it) and his last contribution to the literature of prophecy. It is a testimony to the authenticity of his lifelong occupation of the prophet's office, with its risks of self-delusion and the ever-present threat to sanity and mental balance that it entailed. He recovered enough in his last months to plan a new version of the film *Things to Come*, brought up to date with nuclear weapons;[25] but *Mind at the End of Its Tether* suggests very strongly that prophecy for this writer was, in the end— however much grotesque self-repetition it involved—no joke.

IV

Both the duality of prophecy and the conflicting strains of Wells's personality are mirrored in his fine late work of fiction *The Croquet Player* (1936). In this allegorical 'ghost story' Georgie Frobisher, the selfish and ineffectual croquet player of the title, finds himself hypnotised by the complementary tales of two fellow-guests at the health resort of Les Noupets, Dr Finchatton and Dr Norbert. Finchatton tells how, as resident physician in the fenland district of Cainsmarsh, he came to believe that the area was haunted by the ghosts of a primitive and violent tribal past. Norbert, Finchatton's psychiatrist, dismisses his patient's narrative as a fairy-tale made up to rationalise his intuition that the whole of humanity is on the point of relapsing into savagery. In this story Finchatton, the hag-ridden Cassandra figure, represents the tormented and myth-making imagination of

25 David C. Smith, *H. G. Wells: Desperately Mortal: A Biography* (New Haven and London: Yale University Press, 1986), p. 478.

the young Wells, who like him was a failed professional scientist.[26] Norbert, a domineering Messiah whom Frobisher likens to Thomas Carlyle and to a Hebrew prophet, is the Moses-Wells who talks of salvation through a revolution in human affairs and the birth of a ' "harder, stronger civilization like steel" '.[27] Norbert believes that a vigorous effort will enable humanity to survive the 'Wrath to Come' (p. 77).

To the complacent Frobisher, these are both unpleasantly haunted men. Norbert is possessed by the very disease that he sets out to diagnose; he is a healer driven to try to save the world in the hope of healing himself. These two figures of obsession, the manic and the depressive, the schizophrenic Messiah and the neurotic man of science, are set off against the insouciant croquet player who has no pretensions to foresight and is ruled, instead, by the most insipid of social conventions. Georgie Frobisher, who shares one of Wells's own forenames, may perhaps be seen as a projection of a further side of his author's personality, that of the entertainer, the enthusiastic amateur games-player, and writer of social comedies. (Not only was Wells the son of a cricketer, but two years before *The Croquet Player* his former mistress Odette Keun had lampooned him in an article entitled 'H. G. Wells—The Player'.[28]) Conceivably, Frobisher may be destined to emerge as a sadder and wiser man after hearing Finchatton's Ancient Mariner-like tale and Norbert's sententious warnings. He remains, like Kipps and Mr Polly at the ends of their respective novels, a denizen of a precarious little earthly paradise, but he admits to some anxiety about world events and to not sleeping as well as he used to. Perhaps even this trivial games-player has a strain of prophetic impatience within him?

In 'How I Died', Wells wrote that after living with his 'death-warrant' for some time, he had grown tired of such gloomy preoccupations. ' "Oh! Death. . . . He's a Bore", I said; "I've done with him" ' (p. 184). Forty years later, the Croquet Player concludes his narrative in much the same way: ' "I don't care. The world *may* be

26 Wells had failed his final examinations at South Kensington, thus terminating an initially promising academic career which might have led on to research.

27 H. G. Wells, *The Croquet Player: A Story* (London: Chatto & Windus, 1936), p. 76. Subsequent page references in text.

28 Odette Keun, 'H. G. Wells—The Player', *Time and Tide* (13–27 October 1934), pp. 1249–51, 1307–09, 1346–48.

going to pieces. The Stone Age may be returning. This may, as you say, be the sunset of civilization. I'm sorry, but I can't help it this morning. I have other engagements. All the same—laws of the Medes and Persians—I am going to play croquet with my aunt at half-past twelve today" ' (p. 82). Yet another experiment in prophecy has taken fire, briefly illuminating the darkness around it, and then fizzled out—a unique individual who has turned into a self-parody. In a famous passage written right at the beginning of his career, Wells describes science in very similar terms to these, but he might equally be predicting the failure of prophecy:

> Science is a match that man has just got alight. He thought he was in a room—in moments of devotion, a temple—and that his light would be reflected from and display walls inscribed with wonderful secrets and pillars carved with philosophical systems wrought into harmony. It is a curious sensation, now that the preliminary sputter is over and the flame burns up clear, to see his hands lit and just a glimpse of himself and the patch he stands on visible, and around him, in place of all that human comfort and beauty he anticipated—darkness still.[29]

29 H. G. Wells, 'The Rediscovery of the Unique', in *Early Writings in Science and Science Fiction*, ed. Robert M. Philmus and David Y. Hughes (Berkeley: University of California Press, 1975), pp. 30–31.

CHAPTER THREE

Possibilities of Space and Time
(*The Time Machine*)

I

Towards the end of *The Time Machine*, the Traveller finishes the story of his adventures, pauses, and looks around at his listeners. He is like a lecturer waiting for the first question after his talk, and like many nervous lecturers he tries to start the ball rolling by interrogating the audience himself. ' "No. I cannot expect you to believe it" ', he begins. ' "Take it as a lie—or a prophecy. Say I dreamed it in the workshop. . . . Treat my assertion of its truth as a mere stroke of art to enhance its interest. And taking it as a story, what do you think of it?" ' (§12). There is another awkward silence, while the Time Traveller fiddles with his pipe, and the audience shift uneasily in their chairs. Then the newspaper editor says that their host ought to be a writer of stories. The narrator, who is not sure what to think, returns to the Traveller's house in Richmond the next day, just in time to speak with him before he departs on the second voyage, from which he never returns. As Robert Philmus has observed, within the narrative framework it is the Traveller's second disappearance and failure to return that proves the reality of time travel, establishing him as a prophet rather than a liar.[1]

For the narrator in the 'Epilogue', the Time Traveller's tale appears as a brief moment of enlightenment, like the flaring of the match in 'The Rediscovery of the Unique', amid the vast ignorance and darkness of the future. The light of prophecy is also the light of science—but it is the extent of the blackness that terrifies. Wells says something very similar in *The Future in America*, when he speaks of the loss of his belief in the imminence of the Christian apocalypse during his adolescence. The study of biology revealed to him an 'endless vista of years ahead' (p. 10). Space, too, appeared as an

1 Robert M. Philmus, 'The Logic of "Prophecy" in *The Time Machine*' in Bernard Bergonzi, ed., *H. G. Wells: A Collection of Critical Essays* (Englewood Cliffs, N.J.: Prentice-Hall, 1976), pp. 67–68.

endless vista, and it is notable that in his early works Wells often uses the word figuratively to indicate a measure of time, as in the phrase 'a space of time'.[2] The complementarity of space and time in the Wellsian universe is summed up in the title of his 1899 volume of stories, *Tales of Space and Time*.

But travel in time with its prophetic associations engages Wells's imagination more intensely than journeys into space. Despite his reputation as the founder of modern science fiction, he took little or no interest in the fiction of spaceships and stellar travel. His rhetorical vision in *The Discovery of the Future* of beings who 'shall laugh and reach out their hands amid the stars' (p. 36) was to inspire other writers, though it corresponds to very little in Wells's own output. Apart from the mystical dream-narrative of his short story 'Under the Knife', *The First Men in the Moon* is his only narrative of a journey beyond the earth's atmosphere; and it is notable that Bedford, the narrator, experiences the dissolution of identity in 'infinite space' during the comparatively short return journey from the moon. He recounts this phase of his adventures in a detached, almost serene way, very different from the Time Traveller's 'hysterical exhilaration' (§3) as he rushes into the future. There is fear and trembling in Wells's imagination of time travel; in *The First Men in the Moon*, however, the experience of thrilling revelation is reserved not for the journey but for the discoveries that the two explorers make on the moon.

What, then, was the source of the exhilaration of time travel? It reflects the bias of Wells's scientific interests, in evolutionary biology and palaeontology rather than astronomy and physics, but it also has a more personal appeal, reflecting his imaginative 'impatience'. We can hardly avoid relating it both to the religious millennialism of his upbringing,[3] and to his intimations of an early death. The fundamental commonsense objection to time travel is the one put forward by Wells's fellow-novelist Israel Zangwill, writing about *The Time Machine* in his *Pall Mall Magazine* column in September 1895. To travel forward more than a few years in time, Zangwill argued, is to travel through one's own death.[4] (It is also, one might add, to travel

2 See, for example, *The Time Machine*, §§ 3 and 4; 'How I Died', p. 182.

3 See Norman and Jeanne Mackenzie, *The Time Traveller: The Life of H. G. Wells* (London: Weidenfeld & Nicolson, 1973), especially pp. 24, 121–24.

4 Israel Zangwill, 'Without Prejudice', reprinted in Patrick Parrinder, ed., *H. G. Wells: The Critical Heritage*, pp. 40–42.

through the death of the machine: metal fatigue and corrosion are often swifter processes than the decay of the human body.) Admittedly, the idea of 'travelling through' death is misleading, since what the time machine achieves for its rider is the circumvention and bypassing of the ravages of time. Since he is still alive and has only aged by a few hours when he reaches 802,701, his journey takes place in a different time-frame from the one that he leaves behind and later re-enters.[5] Wells is aware of some at least of the paradoxes that beset all time-travel narratives. These are most obtrusive at the end of the story, when the narrator returns to Richmond the day after the Traveller's return and sees the Time Machine in the empty laboratory before meeting its inventor in the smoking-room. The Traveller has already passed through this moment in the empty laboratory twice, once on his journey forwards and once on his return journey; on the latter occasion he ' "seemed to see Hillyer . . . but he passed like a flash" ' (§12). If Hillyer is the narrator (as Geduld suggests),[6] the Traveller is seeing him either at this moment or on the occasion, somewhat later, when the narrator re-enters the laboratory. On that second occasion, the narrator catches sight of the ghostly figure of the Traveller on the machine, in the act of departure—or arrival—or both. There are further complications that could be teased out from the story's opening-up of such paradoxes.[7]

Before receiving his 'death warrant' after his footballing accident in 1887, Wells had written 'A Vision of the Past'. Immediately after it, he wrote 'The Chronic Argonauts', the first version of *The Time Machine*, which is set in present time. At the end of 'The Chronic Argonauts' the Reverend Elijah Cook returns from an involuntary voyage into the future, but we never hear his tale of what happened there. Wells's friends complained about the abrupt ending, but it was many years before he was able to write the promised sequel to his own satisfaction. When it eventually appeared in book form, it had been revised at least half a dozen times.[8] For six years (1888–94), we

5 Recent discussions of this question include those by Roslynn D. Haynes in *H. G. Wells: Discoverer of the Future* (London and Basingstoke: Macmillan, 1980), p. 58, and by Harry M. Geduld in *The Definitive 'Time Machine': A Critical Edition of H. G. Wells's Scientific Romance*, ed. Geduld (Bloomington and Indianapolis: Indiana University Press, 1987), pp. 96–97.

6 *The Definitive 'Time Machine'*, p. 118.

7 See ibid., p. 120, n.6.

8 Geoffrey West, *H. G. Wells: A Sketch for a Portrait*, pp. 288–94.

may say, Wells had hesitated on the brink of a genuinely prophetic narrative. His exultation once he had succeeded in giving the future a body and shape is perhaps mirrored in the pun (supposing it is a pun) in Section 4 of *The Time Machine*, when the Traveller reflects on the 'oddness of wells still existing'.

In 'The Chronic Argonauts' there are two narratives, which Wells calls 'exoteric' and 'esoteric'. The exoteric or external story is told by 'the author' (that is, Wells himself), while the esoteric or internal one is told, in an incomplete and fragmentary form, by the Reverend Elijah Cook. The figure who never tells his story is Nebogipfel, the inventor of the time machine or 'Chronic Argo' himself. He only expounds the principles of time-travelling, in conversation with Elijah Cook. In the *National Observer* version of Wells's tale, published between March and June 1894, Nebogipfel, now rechristened or relabelled the Time Traveller, is constantly interrupted by his hearers. His mixture of philosophical argument and adventure narrative is punctuated by commentaries and outbursts of scepticism. The sheer imaginative power of his tale is never given full rein, as if some inhibition still curbed its author. As storytelling, this version is bungled just as 'The Chronic Argonauts' is bungled.[9] But in the final version Wells's inhibitions are overcome, and, once we are with the Traveller on his voyage, the smoking-room setting of the tale is forgotten for very long stretches. The Delphic voice pours forth at last. The Traveller is now more than a mere narrative device. He is a heroic figure within the confines of the story, as well as an avatar of the visionary personality that Wells was discovering, with growing confidence, within himself.

II

When Dr Nebogipfel's unwilling passenger, the Rev. Elijah Cook, arrives back from his journey in 'The Chronic Argonauts' he announces that he has several depositions to make. These concern a murder in the year 1862 (indicating that, unlike the Time Traveller, the Argonauts have gone both ways in time), an abduction in 4003 and a series of ' "assaults on public officials in the years 17,901 and 2" '.[10] In the *National Observer* 'Time Machine', the world of the Eloi

9 'The Chronic Argonauts' and the '*National Observer* Time Machine' are reprinted in *The Definitive 'Time Machine'*, pp. 135–52 and 154–74 respectively.

10 *The Definitive 'Time Machine'*, p. 145.

and Morlocks is set in AD 12,203. In the final version, the date, conveniently registered on the Time Machine's instrument panel, is 802,701. There follows the 'Further Vision', in which the Traveller journeys forward another twenty-nine million years. The reader of the different versions of *The Time Machine* succumbs to the spell of these mysterious numbers themselves—above all, the puzzling figure 802,701—but, beyond that, the meaning of such vast expanses of imaginary time calls out for explanation.

When the Time Traveller's guests encounter the idea of visiting the future, it is plain how limited their (and, by extension, our) horizons are. The Journalist dubs their host 'Our Special Correspondent in the Day after To-morrow' (§2). The Editor wants a tip for next week's horse-racing. The Very Young Man suggests investing some money and travelling forward to collect the profits. Yet even the relatively modest *National Observer* voyage crossed a timespan of more than twice as long as recorded history. Wells's familiarity with the prehistoric vistas opened up by nineteenth-century geology and archaeology had shaped his vision of time travel. As a South Kensington student, he belonged to the first generation of young people to learn as a matter of course about the Stone Age, the era of the dinosaurs, and the formation of the earth. This marvellous new field of knowledge, which rapidly became a staple of popular culture, is evoked in the Epilogue to *The Time Machine* where the narrator imagines the Traveller voyaging into Palaeolithic, Jurassic and Triassic times.

Humanity emerged at a relatively late point in the evolutionary chain, yet our race is still almost unimaginably old. In Wells's next scientific romance, Dr Moreau reminds the narrator that ' "Man has been a hundred thousand [years] in the making" ' (Ch. 14). Actually, Moreau's figure is a gross underestimate, as the chronological horizon of *The Time Machine* hints. In *The Outline of History*, Wells was to put the emergence of the subhuman *pithecanthropus erectus* at six hundred thousand years ago, though since the advent of radio-carbon dating this has been increased to 1.8 million years.[11] In September 1994 reports appeared of the discovery of a fruit-eating humanoid creature (possibly analogous to the Eloi on the evolutionary scale) said to be 4.4 million years old.

Before *The Time Machine* Wells had implied a possible chronology

11 Henry Gee, 'What's our line?', *London Review of Books*, 16:2 (27 January 1994), p. 19.

for future evolution in 'The Man of the Year Million'. Then, in a discussion of 'The Rate of Change in Species' (December 1894), he outlined the considerations that may have led him to lengthen the Time Traveller's journey from the ten thousand years of the *National Observer* version to eighty times as long. Wells claimed it was a little-noticed biological fact that the rate of possible change was governed by the gap between generations, and hence by the average age of maturity in a species. Evolution by natural selection—the strictly Darwinian model to which Wells and Huxley adhered—could not have brought about significant changes within the human species within recorded history, so that any such changes must be cultural, not natural in origin. Wells was determined to show the results of hypothetical natural evolution, not of artificial or eugenic processes in *The Time Machine*. The Traveller's voyage through the best part of a million years thus reflects both the probable age of the human species, in the understanding of Wells's contemporaries, and the minimum time needed for natural selection to produce new degenerate beings descended from present-day humanity.

The time-horizon of Wells's story is also affected by contemporary physical predictions of the future of the solar system. The Traveller reaches a point where not only humanity, but the sun's heat itself is manifestly on the wane. If the story of evolution pointed to the plasticity of biological species, Lord Kelvin's Laws of Thermodynamics portrayed the universe as a finite enclosure in which energy was limited. As a student, Wells had once engaged in a spoof demonstration of a perpetual motion machine (powered by a concealed electromagnet)[12]—a thermodynamic impossibility not unlike a time machine, since both depend on the ability to bypass the normal framework of what, in a lost article, he had called the 'Universe Rigid'.[13] The Second Law of Thermodynamics with its statement that energy always tends to disperse made it clear that the sun and other stars must eventually cool and burn out. *The Time Machine* reflects this entropic process, as well as Sir George Darwin's calculations of the effects of tidal drag on the earth's motion. Later in his life, however, Wells readily admitted that his astronomical predictions had been too gloomy.[14] The study of radioactivity had

12 Geoffrey West, *H. G. Wells: A Sketch for a Portrait*, p. 61.

13 See H. G. Wells, 'Preface', *The Time Machine* (New York: Random House, 1931), p. ix.

14 Ibid., pp. ix–x.

revealed that the source of the sun's heat was thermonuclear fusion rather than combustion; the sun was not a coal fire, so to speak, but a nuclear reactor. The predicted life of the solar system increased from the implied timescale of the 'Further Vision' to ten thousand million years, or perhaps a million million years.[15]

These are unimaginable and almost meaningless expanses of time, yet paradoxically *The Time Machine* renders a thirty million-year future thinkable. That is the 'virtual reality' effect of the story's mythical, apocalyptic hold over the reader. To ask how Wells manages it is to come up against the truism that our only models for imagining the future derive from our knowledge and understanding of the past. He could write of travelling one million or thirty million years ahead only in the light of the geologists' consensus that the earth was already much older than that, though precisely how much older was a matter of conjecture. Kelvin had estimated that the age of the oldest rocks was as little as twenty-five million years, while T. H. Huxley guessed at four hundred million. Summing up the controversy in *The Outline of History*, Wells is unable to arbitrate between these two. Reusing one of his favourite metaphors, he adds that 'Not only is Space from the point of view of life and humanity empty, but Time is empty also. Life is like a little glow, scarcely kindled yet, in these void immensities' (p. 8). In *The Time Machine* he had slightly prolonged that little glow.

III

Wells's use of geological chronology does not explain how he was able to depict the sub-civilisation of the Eloi and Morlocks at a precise date in the future, given in the final version as 802,701. Readers have often wondered why he settled on this curious figure. We may approach an answer by looking more closely at the sensations of time-travelling described in the story. Riding into the future, the Traveller observes the speeding-up of natural phenomena: the alternation of night and day until the two are indistinguishable, the flickering change of the seasons, the swift growth and disappearance of trees. This part of his narrative, which has the vertiginous effect of a constantly accelerating film, may make us wonder how fast he is travelling and how 'long' his journey takes. At one point he mentions a speed of more than a year a minute, but if this were his average velocity it would take nearly eighteen months to reach

15 See H. G. Wells, *The Discovery of the Future*, p. 17 n.6.

802,701. Travelling more rapidly later in the story, he approaches the 'Further Vision' at a speed of something like fifty years per second; but, in fact, five hundred years per second would be a more plausible average speed.[16] At that rate he could have reached the age of the Eloi and Morlocks in less than half an hour.

During his voyage he sees signs of changing civilisations as well as changing natural phenomena. ' "I saw huge buildings rise up faint and fair, and pass like dreams" ', he reports (§3). How often did this happen? ' "I saw great and splendid architecture rising about me, more massive than any buildings of our own time, and yet, as it seemed, built of glimmer and mist" '. There would have been no need to go forward three-quarters of a million years in order to see the architecture of successive human civilisations. Our knowledge of past history suggests that 800 years might have been enough. Even given vastly more durable building materials, 8000 years would have been amply sufficient. Assuming some degree of continuity in human civilisation, changes in architecture would normally take place far more frequently than the natural climatic changes that the Traveller also observes—' "I saw a richer green flow up the hillside, and remain there without any wintry intermission" ' (§3)—let alone the species modifications that have produced the Eloi and Morlocks.

The order of the figures in 802,701 suggests a suitably entropic and cyclical 'running-down' number.[17] We can explain how Wells may have arrived at it, however, by the supposition that *The Time Machine* embodies not one future timescale but two. The two scales, those of historical time measured by the rise and fall of cultures and civili-

16 'Fifty years per second', because the dials of the Time Machine are calibrated in days, thousands of days, millions of days, and thousands of millions, and the Traveler reports that the 'thousands hand was sweeping round as fast as the seconds hands of a watch' (§11). If one complete revolution of the 'thousands' dial represents a million days, he is covering a million days a minute, or 46 years per second—but it would still take more than a week to traverse 30 million years. We may, of course, find the references to the dials highly implausible, especially as the time to be measured is not linear. If the dials measure terrestrial days, one must wonder how they cope with or allow for the slowing down of the terrestrial day to the point where a single solar revolution 'seemed to stretch through centuries' (§11)!

17 Cf. William Bellamy, *The Novels of Wells, Bennett and Galsworthy 1890–1910* (London: Routledge & Kegan Paul, 1971), p. 221.

sations, and of biological time measured by the evolution and devolution of the species, are superimposed upon one another. To begin with, I suggest that Wells must have projected the invention of the Time Machine forward to the beginning of the twentieth century, so that the dinner party at Richmond may be imagined as taking place in 1901. (Analogously, the events of *The War of the Worlds*—which Wells began writing immediately after *The Time Machine* was published—also take place 'early in the twentieth century' (I,1).) He had already used the early twentieth century as baseline in 'The Chronic Argonauts', where the furthest point that we know to have been reached is the years 17,901–02: that is, a voyage of 16,000 years. In *The Time Machine* the world of the Eloi and Morlocks is located not 16,000 but 800,800 years after 1901—a significantly bifurcated number. The 800 years, enough to allow for the rise and fall of a civilisation or two in historical time, take us to 2701. To this figure Wells added a further 800,000 (that is, the best part of a million years) of evolutionary time. Supposing the number 802,701 to have been determined by a process such as this, its poetic appeal as a symbol of entropy would have ensured its adoption. Its significance—to be further explored in Chapter Five below—is that *The Time Machine* is plotted with both timescales, the evolutionary and the historiographic, in mind, though these are incompatible in certain respects. Without the 800-year timescale we cannot easily explain such crucial details as the survival of unmistakably classical forms of architecture into the far future, creating an essentially familiar landscape dominated by the Sphinx and surrounded by ruined palaces and gardens.

IV

The Sphinx and the decaying palaces are central to the symbolism of the story. The Sphinx is the symbol of foreboding and prophecy. The palaces and gardens suggest the landscape of neoclassical paintings and country houses, while alluding to a line of English utopian romances which would have been fresh in the minds of Wells's first readers: Richard Jefferies' *After London* (1885), W. H. Hudson's *A Crystal Age* (1887), and, above all, William Morris's *News from Nowhere* (1890). Morris's death in 1896 drew an affectionate if patronising acknowledgment from Wells in the *Saturday Review*— 'His dreamland was no futurity, but an illuminated past', Wells wrote[18]—but a more wholehearted tribute, and one which hints at the strong connections between *News from Nowhere* and *The Time Machine*, appears at the beginning of *A Modern Utopia*:

> Were we free to have our untrammelled desire, I suppose we should follow Morris to his Nowhere, we should change the nature of man and the nature of things together; we should make the whole race wise, tolerant, noble, perfect . . . in a world as good in its essential nature, as ripe and sunny, as the world before the Fall. But that golden age, that perfect world, comes out into the possibilities of space and time. In space and time the pervading Will to Live sustains for evermore a perpetuity of aggressions.[19]

Chapter Five of *The Time Machine* in the first edition is titled 'In the Golden Age'. In Wells's vision, the 'possibilities of space and time' are not unlimited. In space and time what appears to be a Morrisian utopia can only be fatally flawed; no earthly paradise of this sort is possible. The words Eloi and Morlocks signify angels and devils, and the two races, the products of natural selection, are held together in a predatory and symbiotic relationship—a 'perpetuity of aggressions' without which neither could flourish.

The Time Machine is both an explicitly anti-utopian text, and one which deliberately recalls *News from Nowhere* at a number of points. Morris's pastoral, idyllic society is centred on Hammersmith in West London, while the society of the Eloi is centred two or three miles upstream at Richmond. Both are placed in a lush parkland replacing the nineteenth-century industrial and suburban sprawl beside the River Thames. The Eloi, like the inhabitants of Nowhere and of most other contemporary socialist utopias, eat together in communal dining halls. William Guest, Morris's 'time traveller', learns about the history of twentieth- and twenty-first century England from an old man at the British Museum, while Wells's Traveller journeys to the Palace of Green Porcelain, an abandoned museum of the arts and sciences modelled on the Crystal Palace and the South Kensington

18 H. G. Wells, 'The Well at the World's End', in *H. G. Wells's Literary Criticism*, p. 112.

19 H. G. Wells, *A Modern Utopia* (London: Chapman & Hall, 1905), p. 7. Subsequent page references in text.

Museum.[20] On the evening of his first day with the Eloi, the Traveller climbs to a hilltop, surveys the countryside and exclaims ' "Communism" ' (§4) to himself. The Communism he has in mind must be the pastoral utopia of Morris and Thomas More, rather than the revolutionary industrial society of Marx and Saint-Simon.

On two occasions the Time Traveller mocks at the artificiality of utopian narratives, as if to establish the superior authenticity of his own story. A ' "real traveller" ', he protests, has no access to the vast amount of detail about buildings and social arrangements to be found in these books (§5). He has ' "no convenient cicerone in the pattern of the Utopian books" ' (§5); instead, he has to work everything out for himself by trial and error. The emphasis is not on the exposition of a superior utopian philosophy but on the Traveller's own powers of observation and his habits of deductive and inductive reasoning. In terms of narrative structure as well as of evolutionary possibility, Wells claims to present a less self-indulgent, more realistic vision than Morris and his tradition could offer—as if the world of 802,701 were somehow less of a wish-fulfilment fantasy than Morris's Nowhere. The Time Traveller shows himself in the opening chapters to be a master of several sciences. He is a brilliant inventor and engineer, who is able by his own efforts to test the practical consequences of his theoretical discoveries in four-dimensional geometry.[21] He understands the principles of biology and psychology, and in studying the Eloi and Morlocks without the benefit of a guide he finds himself in the position of an anthropologist and ethnographer. Like an ethnographer in the field, he learns the language of his hosts and attempts to question them about 'taboo' topics such as the mysterious wells dotted across the countryside. At

20 This was the nineteenth-century name for what are now four separate museums clustered together in South Kensington: the Geological Museum, the Natural History Museum, the Science Museum and the Victoria and Albert Museum. It is to this Museum (not the district of London in which it is located) to which the Time Traveller refers when he describes the Palace of Green Porcelain as a ' "latter-day South Kensington" ' (§8).

21 The Time Traveller's discovery is that the fourth dimension is *Time*. In this he anticipates Einstein. The widespread popular view of the fourth dimension in the late nineteenth century was of an extra dimension of space, corresponding to the 'spirit world' and frequented by ghosts. See Michio Kaku, *Hyperspace: A Scientific Odyssey Through Parallel Universes, Time Warps, and The Tenth Dimension* (New York and Oxford: Oxford University Press, 1994), especially p. 84.

each stage, but always aware that he may lack some crucial information, he attempts to theorise his findings.[22] In a characteristic Wellsian touch, he reverses the usual relations between a nineteenth-century anthropologist and his subject-matter, comparing his account of the Eloi to the ' "tale of London which a negro, fresh from Central Africa, would take back to his tribe" '—though he adds that the negro would find plenty of willing informants, and in any case, ' "think how narrow the gap between a negro and a white man of our own times, and how wide the interval between myself and these of the Golden Age!" ' (§5).

Admittedly, the Traveller often fails to live up to his ideal of scientific detachment. Unlike the utopias against which he is reacting, Wells's tale is a violent adventure story as well as something resembling a fieldwork report. The Traveller's behaviour in moments of crisis is typically hysterical, panic-stricken, negligent and, when he confronts the Morlocks, ruthless and desperate. In all this he embodies what Wells in *A Modern Utopia* was to call the Will to Live. Equally, the bloodthirstiness of Wells's anti-utopian realism invites the rejoinder that William Morris made in his review of Edward Bellamy's urban, collectivist utopia *Looking Backward*: 'The only safe way of reading a utopia is to consider it as the expression of the temperament of its author'.[23] *The Time Machine* debunks the utopian dream (a dream that would be reinstated in many of Wells's later works) en route to the discovery that the human species is engaged in a brutal struggle for survival which, in the long run, it cannot win—since all terrestrial life is doomed to extinction. Wells enables his Time Traveller to circumvent his own natural death—to cheat death, so to speak—only to inflict violent death on some of humanity's remote descendants, before going on to witness the collective death of the species and the environment that has sustained it.

In speaking of authorial temperament, Morris was invoking one of the principal categories of late nineteenth-century literary theory. He would have been aware of the widespread reaction against the claims to scientific objectivity made by the realist and naturalist movements; every work of art, it was argued, betrayed the imprint of

---

22 On two occasions his explanations make use of the contemporary anthropological concept of ' "savage survivals" ' (§4).

23 William Morris, 'Looking Backward', *Commonweal* (22 June 1889), p. 194.

its maker's personality.[24] To modern readers, once we have acknow-ledged the complexity and uniqueness of a text like *The Time Machine*, such appeals to personality and temperament have come to seem tautologous rather than illuminating. Nevertheless, we may say that when Wells's artistic imagination was at its most vivid, in the early scientific romances, it was also at its most violent. Ten years after the searing anti-utopianism of these books, he was ready to present his own, comparatively pacific vision of *A Modern Utopia*. As it happens, this apparent change of heart runs parallel with a dramatic improvement in his medical condition.

The cannibalistic Morlocks, the bloodsucking Martians and the bath of pain in which the vivisectionist Dr Moreau transforms wild animals into sham human beings were all conceived during the years in which Wells himself was often bedridden and spitting blood. Since tuberculosis had been (wrongly) diagnosed, it is significant that the first of the Eloi whom the Time Traveller meets face to face has the ' "hectic beauty" ' of a ' "consumptive" ' (§3). The Traveller feels intensely for this society of doomed consumptives, and, once he is armed with a rusty iron bar, he does his best to wreak havoc among the species that lives off them. Wells suffered a final serious relapse in 1898, after the completion of his early romances. He moved to the south coast and commissioned the architect Charles Voysey to build him a house on the cliffs at Sandgate, designed to accommodate the wheelchair to which he soon expected to be confined. But this soon became irrelevant to the needs of its resilient and indeed hyperactive owner.

As his self-identification with the consumptive Eloi came to seem groundless, so did the calculations of planetary cooling reflected in both *The Time Machine* and *The War of the Worlds* lose their sway over contemporary scientific opinion. In *The Interpretation of Radium* (1908)—the book which led Wells to envisage the possibility of atomic warfare—Frederick Soddy wrote that 'Our outlook on the physical universe has been permanently altered. We are no longer the inhabitants of a universe slowly dying from the physical exhaustion of its energy, but of a universe which has in the internal energy of its material components the means to rejuvenate itself

24 One influential expression of this view was Henry James's essay 'The Art of Fiction' (1884). See *Henry James, Selected Literary Criticism*, ed. Morris Shapira (London: Heinemann, 1963), p. 66.

perennially over immense periods of time'.[25] Wells's switch shortly before the First World War from entropic pessimism to a position much closer to Soddy's thermonuclear optimism followed his discovery of the internal energy and potential for self-renewal of his own body, so that he was doubly removed from the outlook of the author of *The Time Machine*.

V

However anti-utopian its outcome, the Time Traveller's voyage confirms that a kind of utopia had been achieved in the 'nearer ages', when, for example, disease had been stamped out, the processes of natural decay slowed if not halted, and population growth brought under control. Nature had been subjugated—for a time (§4). There emerged the monumental civilisation whose buildings and land-scapes still dominated the age of the Eloi and Morlocks. It is the Traveller's fate to chart the seemingly inevitable decline that followed once the human species had reached its zenith, or what the narrator terms the 'manhood of the race' (Epilogue). Pursuing Wells's deterministic hypothesis of a necessary downward curve in human fortunes, he is a symbolic figure embarking on the central quest of the scientific romance, the journey towards, and beyond, the 'last man'.[26]

The Time Traveller is a variant on the heroes of nineteenth-century Gothic and romantic melodrama. He arrives in the future in the midst of a thunderstorm, but when he discovers that the Morlocks have removed his machine his elation gives way to a frenzy of despair. His violent emotionalism is reminiscent of *Frankenstein*—a literary model which Wells acknowledged[27]—and, since Mary Shelley's romance is subtitled *The Modern Prometheus* in allusion to Prometheus's legendary role as the creator of humanity, it is inter-

25 Frederick Soddy, *The Interpretation of Radium: Being the Substance of Six Free Popular Experimental Lectures Delivered at the University of Glasgow*, 3rd edn. (London: Murray, 1912), p. 248.

26 On 'last man' fictions see Patrick Parrinder, 'From Mary Shelley to *The War of the Worlds; The Thames Valley Catastrophe'*, in David Seed, ed., *Anticipations: Essays on Early Science Fiction and Its Precursors* (Liverpool: Liverpool University Press, 1995), pp. 58–74.

27 See H. G. Wells, preface to *The Scientific Romances of H. G. Wells* (1933), reprinted in *H. G. Wells's Literary Criticism*, pp. 240, 241. Subsequent page references in text.

esting that the Time Traveller has a still better claim to Promethean ancestry. The name Prometheus means 'forethought'.[28] Just as Prometheus was one of the Titans, the Traveller is identified with the race of 'giants' who preceded the Eloi and Morlocks and built the great palaces. The Eloi recognise his semi-divine status when they ask, at the moment of his arrival, if he has come from the sun (p. 39). He brings a box of matches with him, and when they run out he steals another box from the Palace of Green Porcelain. Prometheus stole fire from Zeus and brought it down to earth as a gift concealed in a stalk of fennel, to show his friendship for suffering humanity. But neither the frugivorous Eloi nor the half-blind Morlocks are fit recipients for the gift of fire. Future humanity has degenerated so much that the Traveller's matches are used only as purposeless toys, or in self-defence against the Morlocks. In the end his playing with fire causes reckless destruction including, it would seem, the death of Weena who is the one friend he has made in the new world.

Pursuing the imaginative logic of the Time Traveller's identification with Prometheus, we can come to a possible solution to the mystery of his disappearance on his second voyage. Can it be that— punished for his daring in setting out to discover the future in defiance of the gods—his fate is to remain bound to his machine, condemned to perpetual time-travelling just as Prometheus was bound to a rock and condemned to perpetual torture? All that we know is that the narrator's question, 'Will he ever return?', must be answered in the negative. A life of torture, too, was the fate of another famous figure of Greek legend, with whom the Traveller must also be identified: Oedipus, who answered the riddle of the Sphinx, which was the riddle of human life. What the Traveller instinctively fears as he looks into the Sphinx's sightless eyes is the death of humanity and his own inability to survive in a post-human world: ' "I might seem some old-world savage animal . . . a foul creature to be incontinently slain" ' (§3). But he does not flinch from his self-appointed mission of traversing the valley of the shadow of death and reporting the Shape of Things to Come to the people of his own time: ' "It is how the thing shaped itself to me, and as that I give it to you" ' (§10).

---

28 Robert Graves, *The Greek Myths* (Harmondsworth: Penguin, 1955), I, p. 148.

CHAPTER FOUR
A Sense of Dethronement
The Time Machine
and *The Island of Doctor Moreau*)

I

The Time Traveller comes back from the future haggard, dishevelled and bloodstained. No sooner has he gone upstairs to dress for dinner than his guests begin to vent their astonishment. ' "Does our friend eke out his modest income with a crossing?" ' asks the newspaper editor, ' "or has he his Nebuchadnezzar phases?" ' (§2). The second guess is close to the mark, though its allusion to the Book of Daniel may be lost on most modern readers. Far from doubling as a Dickensian street-sweeper, the Traveller is like the Babylonian king who lost his throne and was forced to eat grass as oxen and make his dwelling with the beasts of the field (Daniel 4: 31–3). Face to face with the Sphinx, the Traveller fears he will be seen as some old-world savage animal; later he feels cut off from his own kind like a ' "strange animal in an unknown world" '(§5). Similarly, the narrator of *The War of the Worlds* observes that, after the Martian invasion, humankind is 'no longer a master, but an animal among the animals'. It is his lot 'to lurk and watch, to run and hide; the fear and empire of man [has] passed away' (II, 6). This feeling of a 'sense of dethronement' (II, 6) is a recurrent nightmare in the early Wells. *The Island of Doctor Moreau, The Time Machine* and *The War of the Worlds* all suggest that the story of Nebuchadnezzar's banishment should be read as a prophetic parable of human destiny.

The loss of human mastery over nature is a source of fear, horror and irony throughout the scientific romances. One may wonder what it was in Wells's outlook and experience that led him to portray the metamorphosis of man into animal with such intensity. Not only was his bodily constitution in the years 1888–1898 weakened by a traumatic illness, but we have his statement in the *Autobiography* that 'until I was over forty the sense of physical inferiority was a constant acute distress which no philosophy could mitigate'.[1] The childhood of at least one of his fictional protagonists—Benham in *The Research Magnificent*, to be discussed below—is dominated by fear of animals. In adult life, Wells's fascination with big cats was expressed in his relationship with Rebecca West; the two lovers named one another Jaguar and Panther.[2] However, his ambivalent feelings towards animals are perhaps most accurately reflected in his scientific interests and choice of a profession, since the practice and enjoyment of dissection are inseparable from good biology teaching. Wells's little-read *Text-Book of Biology* (1893) is virtually a dissection manual. Volume One ('Vertebrata') consists of four sections devoted to the anatomy and physiology of the rabbit, the frog, the dogfish and the amphioxa. In the Wells Collection at the University of Illinois one can see the copy of the *Text-Book* that he presented to Catherine Robbins, his biology student and wife-to-be. Inside it is one of the author's pen-and-ink sketches or 'picshuas', with the figure of a rabbit dissecting a man. This is perhaps the most succinct expression that Wells ever gave to the 'sense of dethronement'.

In the 1933 Preface to his *Scientific Romances*, Wells mentioned not only *Frankenstein* but Apuleius's *Golden Ass* among his literary antecedents (*H. G. Wells's Literary Criticism*, p. 240). Like *The Golden Ass*, which tells of the miseries suffered by a man imprisoned in an ass's body, Wells's conception of human dethronement combines comedy and irony with a ready understanding of the pain and humiliation that we inflict on beings lower in the social and natural hierarchy than ourselves. At the same time, dethronement is a natural process for Wells; it does not need enchantment or a magic trick to bring it about. In this respect, his fiction is a direct expression of the Darwinian vision, as summed up for example in T. H. Huxley's 1863 volume of essays *Man's Place in Nature*. There is little need to

---

1 H. G. Wells, *Experiment in Autobiography: Discoveries and Conclusions of a Very Ordinary Brain (Since 1866)* (London: Gollancz and The Cresset Press, 1966), II, p. 582. Subsequent page references in text.

2 On Wells and big cats see Brian W. Aldiss, 'Wells and the Leopard Lady', in Patrick Parrinder and Christopher Rolfe, eds., *H. G. Wells Under Revision: Proceedings of the International H. G. Wells Symposium, London, July 1986* (Selinsgrove: Susquehanna University Press, and London and Toronto: Associated University Presses, 1990), pp. 27–39; also in Brian W. Aldiss, *The Detached Retina: Aspects of SF and Fantasy* (Liverpool: Liverpool University Press, 1995), pp. 116–27.

elaborate on Wells's profound indebtedness to Huxley, his biology teacher at the Normal School of Science. Wells handsomely acknowledged the debt, which has become a commonplace of biography and criticism.[3] His vision of dethronement both develops and distorts certain elements in the evolutionary outlook of Huxley and Darwin.

II

Darwin's *Origin of Species*, the Bible of the evolutionary idea, ends on a note of resounding optimism. Its author speaks of the grandeur of the new view of nature, in which 'not one living species will transmit its unaltered likeness to a distant futurity', and 'very few will transmit progeny of any kind to a far distant futurity'. He has no fears that humanity, the noblest animal, will not be among those very few. Indeed, 'we may look forward with some confidence to a secure future of great length . . . as natural selection works solely by and for the good of each being, all corporeal and mental endowments will tend to progress towards perfection'.[4]

Darwin gradually lost his religious faith in the years after 1859,[5] and the note of Christian uplift with which he concludes the *Origin* appears to be both self-contradictory and at variance with his theory. The theory of natural selection derives from the Malthusian view of life as a remorselessly competitive struggle for existence. Malthus, in Darwin's words, had demonstrated in his *Essay on the Principle of Population* that 'many more individuals of each species are born than can possibly survive'.[6] ('Survival', in this context, implies the production of offspring.) Evolutionary 'progress', whether or not it moves towards perfection, depends on the premature dying-out of the majority. Wells had imbibed a similar doctrine before he became a biology student from Winwood Reade's popular rationalist history

3 For a partially dissenting view see Leon Stover, 'Applied Natural History: Wells vs. Huxley', in Patrick Parrinder and Christopher Rolfe, eds., *H. G. Wells Under Revision*, pp. 125–33.

4 Charles Darwin, *The Origin of Species by Means of Natural Selection*, 6th edn., (London: Murray, 1910), pp. 402, 403.

5 Charles Darwin, *Autobiography*, (London: Watts, 1929), p. 149. He describes himself as a 'Theist', though no longer an orthodox Christian, at the time of writing the *Origin*.

6 Charles Darwin, *The Origin of Species*, Introduction, p. 3.

The Martyrdom of Man (1872).[7] The narrator of *The War of the Worlds* observes, as he watches the Martians dying from the ravages of terrestrial bacteria, that 'By the toll of a billion deaths man has bought his birthright of the earth, . . . For neither do men live nor die in vain' (II, 8).

Huxley, who did not share Darwin's reticence in matters of faith, turned to what is in many respects a Stoic outlook in reaction against the amorality of the 'cosmic process', and its indifference towards all human ends. His speculative essay 'Evolution and Ethics' and his work on Hume show his readiness to search through the philosophical traditions of East and West for the ancestry of the doctrines which, he felt, arose necessarily from the study of evolution. In 'Evolution and Ethics' he argues that it is only the prospect of subjugating nature through technology which stands between modern humanity and the quietist, world-renouncing attitudes of the ancient Stoics and Hindu philosophers. Formerly, 'ethical man' had to admit that the cosmos was too strong for him; now he has discovered his own, scientific sources of strength. Huxley dissented from the Stoic 'apathy', arguing that human beings must oppose the cosmic process insofar as they could.[8]

Huxley's breadth of vision was an incomparable inspiration to the young Wells, who took his first-year courses in biology and zoology in 1884–85. He described Huxley's course as a 'grammar of form and a criticism of fact', at the end of which he 'had man definitely placed in the great scheme of space and time'.[9] But if Huxley was the classical philosopher of evolution, his pupil was its morbidly romantic poet. This is evident from the contrast between Huxley's late essays and Wells's early science journalism written at much the same time. Huxley's figurative descriptions of the state of nature and the cosmic process are part of a metaphysical argument, while Wells's visionary metaphors often seem to be ends in themselves. Human life is deceptively tranquil, like an eddy in the stream of the

7 In his *H. G. Wells and the World State* (Freeport, N.Y.: Books for Libraries Press, 1971), p. 227, W. Warren Wagar says of Reade's book that 'no other product of the mental climate in which Wells grew to intellectual maturity is so unmistakably "Wellsian" '.

8 T. H. Huxley, *Evolution and Ethics and Other Essays* (London: Macmillan, 1895), pp. 77, 83.

9 H. G. Wells, *Experiment in Autobiography*, I, p. 201; *A Modern Utopia*, p. 376.

universe;[10] science is a match which man has just struck in the dark.[11] What Wells romanticises in his early essays and scientific romances is, time and again, the drama of death and extinction.

The centrality of death and extinction to the evolutionary vision is most spectacularly evident in those great cultural monuments of the late nineteenth century, the natural history museums. These museums grew out of the earlier, jumbled 'Cabinet of Curiosities', described by Wordsworth in the 1805 *Prelude* as a 'gaudy Congress, fram'd / Of things, by nature, most unneighbourly' (3: 651); and they reflect the taxonomic desire to impose system and order upon the huge range of organic life that could be collected and put on public exhibition. By the end of the century, the museums had come to be dedicated to displaying the logic of the evolutionary process through dramatic arrangements of skeletons. The most remarkable example—still preserving, at the time of writing, almost the same arrangement as on the day of its opening—is the gallery of Palaeontology and Comparative Anatomy in the Jardin des Plantes in Paris, constructed in 1898. Here as you enter the main door you see great lines of anatomical specimens marching towards you, as if to represent the very life-force of evolutionary advance—and at the head of them is a sculpted human figure, the one representation of a living creature amid a forest of bones. The history of the Paris Museum of Natural History goes back to 1793. In the English-speaking world, the most influential of the nineteenth-century museums are those at the universities of Oxford, Harvard and Yale, and at South Kensington, where Alfred Waterhouse's great building was opened to the public in April 1881, two years before Wells came to study at the Normal School of Science just across the road.

Waterhouse's Natural History Museum has often been described as a cathedral or temple of science, but it is also a kind of Golgotha, a mausoleum of dead animals. The great halls are filled with stuffed carcases, skeletons, fossils, and in some cases plaster casts. Like all natural history museums, it arouses wonder by exhibiting the range of the extinct as well as the living animal kingdom. The crowd-pulling capacity of dinosaurs was a Victorian discovery, exploited by (among others) the promoters of the Crystal Palace, who erected the plaster reproductions in the lake at Sydenham that can still be seen

10 H. G. Wells, 'The "Cyclic" Delusion', in *Early Writings*, ed. Robert M. Philmus and David Y. Hughes, p. 113.
11 See Chapter 2, n.29 above.

today. (Wells was taken to see them as a child, and in *Kipps* he shows his hero and Ann Pornick courting under the shadow of the Labyrinthodon.) If such displays show the diversity and astonishing resourcefulness of the natural world, they also serve in a more covert way as a *memento mori*, a constant reminder of death both animal and human.

From the beginning the new museums included human bones and skeletons among their most prominent exhibits. According to the *General Guide* to the South Kensington museum published in 1886, human remains were on display in the Palaeontological Collection, the Osteological Gallery and the Introductory Collection in the Central Hall. In the main hall, the centrepiece was the skeleton of a sperm-whale, while Bay I on the west side contained a human skeleton in the same case with two large monkeys. Opposite was a case showing hands and feet including a human hand.[12] In the museums at Oxford and Paris one can still see the original display-cases with human and primate skeletons side by side. These exhibits were there to drive home the proofs of 'man's place in nature' and of his evolutionary descent with maximum impact. They can still produce a sense of shock. The natural history museums had functions beyond that of demonstrating the systematic ordering of the world of nature. They were centres of propaganda for the evolutionary theory, and they were also the one public institution to which anyone could go to contemplate the physical facts of human, not merely animal, life and death.

Wells was not the only nineteenth-century writer to respond to the fascination of these museums. Jules Verne's Captain Nemo has his own museum aboard the submarine *Nautilus*, while Herman Melville's *Moby Dick*, with its exhaustive discussions of the whale and cetological science, itself resembles nothing so much as a vast museum. Melville's explanation that 'To produce a mighty book, you must choose a mighty theme'[13] may also explain why the great, exotic animals such as whales and dinosaurs contribute so powerfully to the appeal of natural history museums. They represent alternatives to human mastery which, however, have been dethroned. (Writing in 1851, Melville perceptively discussed

12 *A General Guide to the British Museum (Natural History), Cromwell Road, London, S.W.* (London: British Museum Trustees, 1886) , pp. 23–24, 34.

13 Herman Melville, *Moby Dick, or The Whale*, World's Classics edn. (Oxford: Oxford University Press, 1920), p. 542.

whether or not the whale faced eventual extermination.) In this respect, Wells, once again, turned the tables on human pride. His Palace of Green Porcelain in *The Time Machine* is an imaginary museum containing the story of human culture, science and technology as well as the whole of earth history; and it is also the last of all museums, marking humanity's forthcoming extinction.

At South Kensington, Wells studied the 'science of life' on the dissecting table and under the microscope. His statement that he 'had man definitely placed in the great scheme of space and time' suggests an organisation of dead forms like that of a museum—a 'Universe Rigid' spread out for inspection.[14] 'Natural selection', he later wrote, 'is selection by Death'.[15] 'The long roll of palaeontology is half filled with the records of extermination'.[16] A selection of the titles of his early science journalism speaks for itself: 'The Duration of Life', 'Death', 'Concerning Skeletons', 'Zoological Retrogression', 'On Extinction', 'Bio-Optimism'. The last title might seem to promise a more sanguine view, but the reality is otherwise: 'As a matter of fact, Natural Selection grips us more grimly than it ever did . . . In our hearts we all wish that the case was not so, we all hate Death and his handiwork; but the business of science is not to keep up the courage of men, but to tell the truth. . . . The names of the sculptor who carves out the new forms of life are, and so far as human science goes at present they must ever be, Pain and Death'.[17] In 'Human Evolution, An Artificial Process' (1896), a short essay published six months after *The Island of Doctor Moreau*, Wells at last offered to guide his readers out of the valley of death presided over by the Calvinistic deity of Natural Selection, declaring that 'in Education lies the possible salvation of mankind from misery and sin'.[18] That was to be

14 'The Universe Rigid' was the title of a lost article of Wells's, rejected by the editor of the *Fortnightly Review* (Frank Harris) in 1891. See *Experiment in Autobiography*, I, pp. 214, 356.

15 H. G. Wells, 'Human Evolution, An Artificial Process', in *Early Writings*, ed. Robert M. Philmus and David Y. Hughes, p. 211.

16 H. G. Wells, 'On Extinction', in ibid., p. 170.

17 H. G. Wells, 'Bio-Optimism', in ibid., pp. 208–09.

18 H. G. Wells, 'Human Evolution, An Artificial Process', in ibid., p. 219. On the chronology of this transition in Wells's thinking, see Robert M. Philmus's comments in *The Island of Doctor Moreau: A Variorum Text*, ed. Philmus (Athens and London: University of Georgia Press, 1993), pp. xvii, xxxix.

the creed of the later Wells, for whom the vision of human dethronement was no longer quite so compelling.

III

The Island of Doctor Moreau portrays the scientist as villain. The three
Europeans at the heart of the story, Moreau, Montgomery and the
narrator Prendick, all have some training in biology or medicine, but
Moreau is unique in pursuing biological theories and acting in a
scientific spirit. Once a prominent English physiologist, his experiments on live animals were exposed by an investigative journalist,
forcing him to flee the country. He moved his laboratory to a remote
and uninhabited Pacific island, taking Montgomery—who had been
disgraced as a result of some unspecified, possibly homosexual,
lapse—as his assistant. In the figure of Moreau, Wells was reflecting
on the controversy over vivisection, which in the eighteen-nineties
was already more than a quarter of a century old. Many earlier
novels had dealt with the topic, including Wilkie Collins's *Heart and
Science* (1883).

Prendick, who reaches the island after his life has been saved by
Montgomery, dimly remembers the pamphlet detailing the 'Moreau
horrors'. The physiologist's sinister demeanour and the secrecy
surrounding his experiments on the island readily identify him with
the literary tradition of the lone, demonic researcher. Nevertheless,
his outlook is not totally removed from that of more orthodox
scientists. Before he left England he published regularly in scientific
journals and engaged (with 'brutal directness', admittedly) in public
discussion (Ch. 7). Prendick feels that the scientific community
ought perhaps to have rallied round Moreau at the time of his
disgrace; this may be read as an oblique comment, on Wells's part,
on the literary world's failure in 1895 to support Oscar Wilde.[19]
Moreau's outline of the theory behind his experiments overlaps to a
considerable extent with one of Wells's contemporary scientific
articles, 'The Limits of Individual Plasticity'. When he tells Prendick
that ' "The study of Nature makes a man at last as remorseless as
Nature" ' (Ch. 14)—a suitably spinechilling statement in its fictional
context—Moreau echoes what might well be said of more orthodox
biological and surgical practices. The removal of a gangrened limb,

19 Wells acknowledged Wilde's disgrace as an influence on the writing
on *Moreau* in his preface to the Atlantic edition of the novel. *The Atlantic
Edition of the Works of H. G. Wells* (London: Unwin, 1924), II, p. ix.

and even the pulling of teeth, demand a certain ruthlessness. The pain that Moreau's animals suffer may have been the lot of most human beings at some point in their lives before the discovery of anaesthetics. One of the twentieth century's most humane physiologists, J. B. S. Haldane, sounded a little like Moreau when he concluded a discussion of the prospects of genetic engineering by affirming that 'The scientific worker of the future will more and more. . . [become] conscious of his ghastly mission and proud of it'.[20]

Moreau regards himself not only as a scientist but as a ' "religious man . . . as every sane man must be" ' (Ch. 14). His is an evolutionary religion that allows him to disregard merely humanitarian considerations in the name of a spiritual quest to remove the ' "mark of the beast" ' from his experimental subjects. In an article on 'The Province of Pain', Wells had argued that pain might represent a 'limited and transitory' phase in the evolution of life 'from the automatic to the spiritual'.[21] If Moreau is effectively playing God by trying to speed up the evolutionary process, his project of using vivisection to raise animals to the level of civilised men is also a parody of the 'white man's burden' of European imperialism. The most successful of his experiments have produced Beast-Men capable of serving and attending on their European masters, but no more. (One of these, M'ling, is sufficiently trustworthy to accompany Montgomery on his long journey to Arica and back.) Like tribal subjects under colonial rule, the remainder of the Beast Folk accept Moreau's laws and live together in a jungle village. But by the time of Prendick's arrival they have already begun to revert, and seen through his eyes the story of the island is not one of miraculous reclamation and the artificial creation of new forms, but rather of natural degeneration. For some of the time Prendick thinks he is surrounded by deformed men rather than improved animals; he concludes (quite irrationally) that Moreau is vivisecting human beings and that he himself is destined to become an experimental subject. By the end of the novel, not only have the Beast Folk lost nearly all traces of the civilised imprint, but Montgomery has

20 J. B. S. Haldane, *Daedalus: or Science and the Future* (London: Kegan Paul, 1924), pp. 92–93.

21 H. G. Wells, 'The Province of Pain', in *Early Writings*, ed. Robert M. Philmus and David Y. Hughes, pp. 198–99.

succumbed to a form of bestiality and Prendick has been forced to live as an animal among the animals.

The reversion of the Beast Folk, which Prendick observes in the span of a few months, parallels the process of future human degeneration discovered by the Time Traveller; it is effectively a speeded-up version of the devolutionary process.[22] That is why Prendick understands that he sees before him 'the whole balance of human life in miniature' (Ch. 16). He speaks of the 'unspeakable aimlessness of things upon the island' (Ch. 16), and his disorientation and suffering are more intense and more traumatic than were the Time Traveller's. Both tales offer a practical demonstration of the truths about the evolutionary process that Wells had put forward in an 1891 article on 'Zoological Retrogression'. Here he argued that the 'invincibly optimistic' popular view of evolution as a steady ascent was based on a wilful disregard of Nature's shadow side.[23] The article gives numerous examples of the 'fitful and uncertain' nature of evolutionary advance, pointing out that 'rapid progress has often been followed by rapid extinction or degeneration' (p. 167). Wells concludes that human ascendancy is precarious and that some other species— elsewhere he mentions the herring, the frog, the Aphis and the rabbit as possibly having better survival chances than humankind[24]—might emerge to 'sweep *homo* away into the darkness': 'The Coming Beast must . . . be reckoned in any anticipatory calculations regarding the Coming Man' (p. 168).

IV

In *The Time Machine* and *The Island of Doctor Moreau*, Wells presents both the theory and the experience of zoological retrogression and human dethronement. In each book cannibalism appears as a symbol of retrogression. The Morlocks feed off the Eloi, while Prendick and his fellow-survivors almost succumb to cannibalism after the wreck of the *Lady Vain* (a synonym for Dame Nature?). On

---

22 See Robert M. Philmus, *The Island Of Doctor Moreau: A Variorum Text*, p. xxiii, and David Seed, 'Doctor Moreau and his Beast People', *Udolpho* 17 (June 1994), p. 11. Seed notes resemblances between Prendick's description of the Beast Folk and Darwin's discussions of reversion and arrested development in *The Descent of Man* (1871).

23 H. G. Wells, 'Zoological Retrogression', in *Early Writings*, ed. Robert M. Philmus and David Y. Hughes, p. 158. Subsequent page references in text.

24 H. G. Wells, 'The Rate of Change in Species', in ibid., p. 131.

board the *Ipecacuanha*, Montgomery revives Prendick with a dose of 'some scarlet stuff, iced', which tastes like blood (Ch. 2). In the background they can hear the 'low angry growling of some large animal', and soon afterwards Prendick becomes aware of Montgomery's strange assistant. M'ling is dressed in blue overalls, but his appearance and behaviour are stamped inescapably with what the nineteenth century called the Mark of the Beast—though Prendick is not fully aware of this at first. As, semi-conscious, he was carried aboard the *Ipecacuanha*, he registered a 'dark face with extraordinary eyes close to mine' (Ch. 1). Soon the power of M'ling's gaze will bring Prendick to the point of full recognition.

To meet an animal face to face and look it in both eyes is an unusual experience for most people, partly as a result of physical differences and partly because of our preconceptions which prevent us from encountering animals on terms of equality. In *The Time Machine* and *The Island of Doctor Moreau*, Wells imagines animals capable of walking upright. His narrators experience the *frisson* of meeting them on level terms and, as a result, seeing their own bestial nature mirrored in the other. Thus the Time Traveller's first confrontation with a Morlock is marked by a disturbing eye-contact. Exploring a 'colossal ruin' on the fourth day after his arrival in the future, he suddenly finds that he is not alone:

> 'A pair of eyes, luminous by reflection against the daylight without, was watching me out of the darkness.
> 'The old instinctive dread of wild beasts came upon me. I clenched my hands and steadfastly looked into the glaring eyeballs. I was afraid to turn.' (§5)

In this scene, the emotions of fear and horror transmitted through the gaze might remind us of the Traveller's earlier encounter with the sightless eyes of the Sphinx. Facing the Sphinx, it is the Traveller who is seized with panic and tears his eyes away. A moment later, when the first of the Eloi appears, he quickly regains confidence. They seem to meet on terms of equality: ' "He came straight up to me and laughed into my eyes" ' (§4). In retrospect, this outburst of laughter is not a good sign, and such mutual recognition as it implies is very superficial. Unlike the Eloi, the first Morlock to come in contact with the Traveller takes the trouble to scrutinise him intensely. There is a feeling of instant enmity and, as in virtually all his subsequent encounters with the Morlocks, the Traveller's superior aggressiveness defeats his antagonist:

'Overcoming my fear to some extent, I advanced a step and
spoke. I will admit that my voice was harsh and ill-con-
trolled. I put out my hand and touched something soft. At
once the eyes darted sideways, and something white ran past
me.' (§5)

Rightly or wrongly, the Traveller registers the Eloi as a man, and the
Morlock as a beast; and the confrontation with a wild beast is an
archetypal moment in Wells's work. Looking into M'ling's eyes,
which shine with a 'pale green light' in the dark, Prendick is
reminded of the 'forgotten horrors of childhood', and he too feels an
instinctive dread (Ch. 4). Like the Morlock, M'ling looks away first.
Neither is fully able to meet the challenge of the narrator's gaze.
    Chapter 9 of *The Island of Doctor Moreau*, 'The Thing in the Forest', is
a further elaboration of the theme of encountering the beast. The
Leopard Man whom Prendick sees drinking from the stream appears
at first as a man, clothed in the bluish cloth of Moreau's employees—
but going on all-fours. The narrative rhythm of the chapter derives
from the series of eye-contacts between the Leopard Man and
Prendick, whose fear intensifies as he realises that he is being stalked
in the gathering darkness. Once again, however, the Leopard Man
cannot withstand his direct gaze:

> I advanced a step or two looking steadfastly into his eyes.
>   'Who are you?' said I. He tried to meet my gaze.
>   'No!' he said suddenly, and, turning, went bounding away
> from me through the undergrowth. Then he turned and
> stared at me again. His eyes shone brightly out of the dusk
> under the trees.
>   My heart was in my mouth, but I felt my only chance was
> bluff, and walked steadily towards him. He turned again and
> vanished into the dusk. Once more I thought I caught the
> glint of his eyes, and that was all. (Ch. 9)

The glint of his eyes coming and going conveys the mutual suspicion
and what rapidly turns into a power-struggle between Prendick and
the Leopard Man—a theme that extends to Prendick's relations with
all the Beast Folk, and which can be traced through repeated
moments of eye-contact in the succeeding chapters. The tensions of
fear and horror in the story are greatly intensified by these moments.
It is a sign of the emotional ramifications of the theme for Wells that

he was to return to it in a much later novel, rewriting the scene with the Leopard Man in *The Research Magnificent* (1915).

Benham, the protagonist of *The Research Magnificent*, contracts an 'ineradicable' fear of animals when, as a child, his nursemaid brings him face to face with a circus tiger (Prelude, iv). As an adult, his conception of a voluntary aristocracy involves the conquest and subjugation of fear. The decisive test comes on safari in India when, venturing alone into the jungle, he meets a tiger face to face at a water-hole. Benham addresses the beast:

> 'I am Man,' he said, and lifted a hand as he spoke. 'Master. Master. . . .' For a moment man and beast were as still as stone.
>
> His heart leaped within him as the tiger moved. But the great beast went sideways, . . . and stood again watching him.
>
> 'Man,' he said, in a voice that had no sound, and took a step forward.
>
> 'Wough!' With two bounds the monster had become a great grey streak that crackled and rustled in the shadows of the trees. (Prelude, xi)

In this rewriting there is a manifest didactic intention that was absent from Prendick's meeting in the forest. Wells would have known Henry James's novella 'The Beast in the Jungle', in which the metaphorical 'beast' signifies a mental, not physical, challenge to the protagonist's obsessive masculine will-power. Benham 'proves himself' in a literal encounter, showing his fitness to bear the (white) man's burden of mastery over nature, while the beast's cry remains as a strangled dissenting voice like the Leopard Man's 'No!'.

In *The Island of Doctor Moreau*, it is a sign of Prendick's ultimate weakness that he eventually resorts to violence to rid himself of the challenge of the Leopard Man (and, later, of the Hyena—Swine). At the end of Chapter 9 he attacks the Leopard Man with a stone in a sling, and later in the book he draws a revolver and kills the rebellious beast, disregarding Moreau's instructions. Mere will-power is not enough for Prendick, any more than it was for the Time Traveller faced with the Morlocks. The shooting of the Leopard Man is ambiguously presented, since Prendick justifies it by the need to save the creature from further tortures in Moreau's laboratory. Indeed, this rather dubious act of euthanasia occurs at the moment when, Prendick says, he looks at the beast 'with the light gleaming in its eyes' and realises 'the fact of its humanity' (Ch. 16). Nevertheless, his exhilaration after the event suggests not mercy-killing but the satisfaction of a power-lust awoken in the first moment of seeing M'ling and experiencing the forgotten horrors of childhood.

If Moreau also feels the 'old instinctive dread' of wild beasts, he exacts a more terrible revenge upon them by forcing them to act as if they were human beings. Prendick is a sympathetic narrator precisely because he plays a somewhat inglorious role in the story, lacking either the ruthlessness of Moreau or the relentless idealism of a figure like Benham. While his struggle to dominate or at least hold his own among the Beast Folk generates much of the novel's narrative excitement, that struggle largely fails. (Finally it takes the fortuitous arrival of a drifting boat to enable him to escape from the island.) For Prendick the time of dethronement comes after the deaths of Moreau and Montgomery, when he lacks the single-mindedness to set himself up as Moreau's successor. Far from ruling the Beast Folk with a rod of iron he settles for a relationship of parity with them, eating their food, joining in their rituals and, for a time, sharing their huts in the forest. During these last months on the island, he comes to understand their suffering as Moreau never did. Finally, after his return to England, he is a traumatised individual who sees that his fellow-human beings are no better than tormented Beast Folk.

V

Rather like the Time Traveller face to face with the Sphinx, Prendick learns to conceive of human destiny in animal terms. As a result of his experience he loses his faith in the 'sanity of the world' (Ch. 16). But he too has a fleeting moment of prophecy when, at the end of the novel, he predicts that 'presently the degradation of the Islanders will be played over again on a larger scale' (Ch. 22). This vision of inevitable human degeneration is instantly rescinded, as if it were a mere symptom of the psychic damage he has undergone, and the novel's overall pessimism is a little relieved by moments of comedy (as in Prendick's relationship with the Dog Man), and by the serenity he finally achieves through the study of astronomy. Nevertheless, *The Island of Doctor Moreau* enacts the dislodgment and overthrow of any 'artificial process' of education or the rule of law, to which humanity might look for salvation from the natural evolutionary process. Its outbursts of pain and despair elicited an overwhelmingly hostile press reaction at the time of first publication, and continued to embarrass its author in later life. In his preface to the collected edition of his scientific romances in 1933, he wrote that 'Now and then, though I rarely admit it, the universe projects itself towards me in a hideous grimace'. But he sought to defuse the result as an 'exercise in youthful blasphemy' (*H. G. Wells's Literary Criticism*, p. 243).

By 1933, his vision of human dethronement had receded, though it is never entirely absent. *Mr Blettsworthy on Rampole Island* is in some respects a rewriting of *The Island of Doctor Moreau*, and similar themes come to the fore in *The Croquet Player*. After about 1897 Wells largely ceased to write scientific journalism, and there is a distinct poverty of strictly scientific ideas in *The First Men in the Moon* or *The Food of the Gods* as compared with his earlier romances. As he moved from an anti-utopian to an increasingly utopian outlook, he preferred to fix his hopes on the possibility of some form of species 'mutation' to avoid zoological retrogression and ensure survival.

Darwin in *The Origin of Species* had gone beyond Malthus with his principle of natural selection, introduced in these words: 'As many more individuals of each species are born than can possibly survive; and as, consequently, there is a frequent recurrent struggle for existence, it follows that any being, if it vary however slightly in any manner profitable to itself, under the complex and sometimes varying conditions of life, will have a better chance of surviving, and thus be *naturally selected*'.[25] The challenge to the human species, for the later Wells, was to achieve not so much natural as self-selection, by curbing its own regressive and self-destructive tendencies. But Wells continued to express this predicament in naturalistic, evolutionary terms. Here he is describing the 'After-Man' in *The Conquest of Time* (1942):

> I am convinced that the species we call so prematurely *Homo sapiens* is bound to extinguish itself unless it now sets about adapting itself at a great rate to the stresses it has brought down upon itself. But if it does that, then it will become a new species of self-conscious animal. It seems improbable, though it is not impossible, that it will cease to interbreed freely, and so long as it does not do that it will not split into two or more divergent species; it will evolve *en bloc*.[26]

25 Charles Darwin, *The Origin of Species*, Introduction, p. 3.
26 H. G. Wells, *The Conquest of Time*, p. 57.

Wells emphasises that the environment to which the species has to adapt is a self-created environment, and, if it fails, it will be the first known species to 'extinguish itself'. One can see here both Wells's contribution to ecological thinking, and the extent to which he remains wedded to nineteenth-century biological language. The possibility of 'divergent species' emerging in the course of further evolutionary advance suggests that he remains haunted by the retrogressive vision of the early romances, especially *The Time Machine*.

Three years after *The Conquest of Time*, in his grim last book *Mind at the End of Its Tether*, Wells wrote of the earlier volume that 'Such conquering as that book admits is done by Time rather than Man' (p 3). In *Mind at the End of Its Tether* he still looked to the 'After-Man', but with the implication that interbreeding with *Homo sapiens* should no longer be considered likely. The 'new animal', 'better adapted to face the fate that closes in more and more swiftly upon mankind', would 'certainly not be human': 'There is no way out for Man but steeply up or steeply down. Adapt or perish, now as ever, is Nature's inexorable imperative'. He went on to admit that these crude alternatives were intensely unpalatable, and, besides, that humanity or some part of it would not submit quietly to its fate: 'We want to be in at the death of Man and to have a voice in his final replacement by the next Lord of Creation, even if, Oedipus-like, that successor's first act be parricide' (pp. 18–19). As Wells once again found himself under a medical sentence of death, we may judge from these extracts how far he continued to see the universe as a vast *memento mori*, a theatre of martyrdom in what he still hoped would turn out to be the cause of progress.

CHAPTER FIVE
The Fall of Empires

I

In the preface to *Mind at the End of Its Tether*, Wells announced that there was one more book that he wanted to write: 'a study of the *Decline and Fall of Monarchy and Competitive Imperialisms*' (p. vi). Perhaps because he did not live to complete this project, the formative influence of Edward Gibbon's great history of the *Decline and Fall of the Roman Empire* on Wells's imagination and thought has never had due recognition. He has been seen as modelling himself at various times on such Enlightenment thinkers as Diderot, Tom Paine, Swift and Voltaire, but not on Gibbon, even though both men were the authors of universal histories. In fact, Gibbon's presence in some of Wells's later writings, especially *The Outline of History*, is indisputable; but it does not stop there. The Gibbonian vision of imperial decline provides a crucial link between Wells's historiography and his early science fiction.

Twentieth-century science fiction in general resounds with the music of conquest and empire. Galactic imperialism, the discovery and 'seeding' of planetary worlds in and beyond the solar system, is at the heart of the fiction of Isaac Asimov, James Blish, Arthur C. Clarke, Robert Heinlein, Olaf Stapledon and many others, down to the Canopean empire of Doris Lessing and the Hainish Ekumen of Ursula Le Guin. These projections of the future in terms of conquest and hegemony, of foundation and empire or 'first contact' and eventual confederation, are indebted to particular ideas of historiography. The history of the future, however much the future is claimed to be novel and different, is inevitably modelled to a great extent on the history that we already know. In Asimov's *Foundation*, for example, Hari Seldon uses the science of psychohistory to foresee the fall of the Trantorian empire. Seldon's Foundation is intended to minimise the effects of the fall of Trantor, and one of its main tasks is the compilation of the *Encyclopedia Galactica*, a work from which Asimov gives frequent excerpts and which clearly parallels Gibbon's

Decline and Fall.[1] Other modern SF writers such as Blish and A. E. van Vogt modelled their future history series on Oswald Spengler's *The Decline of the West* (1918–22), as Richard D. Mullen has shown.[2] Spengler proclaimed his work as the embodiment of a Copernican revolution in historiography, moving from what he called the 'Ptolemaic system' of conventional Eurocentric history to a supposedly more scientific view which refused to privilege classical or Western culture over the cultures of the East, the Near East, North Africa and pre-Columbian America.[3] The future histories of modern science fiction were able to extend the Copernican analogy even further, by refusing to privilege terrestrial history against that of the rest of the solar system, the galaxy or the universe.

The appearance of *The Decline of the West* coincided with Wells's own attempt to revolutionise popular historiography in *The Outline of History*. Wells's notions of imperialism, particularly in his fiction, have deeply affected every subsequent writer in the tradition of galactic imperialism; above all, in *The War of the Worlds* he pioneered the story of a hostile invasion of the earth by immeasurably powerful aliens from another planet. But Spengler and Wells differ very sharply over the nature of imperialism. For Spengler, the building of empires heralds the beginning of the decline of a civilisation: its dynamic is now directed outwards rather than inwards, and its forms begin to petrify. Spengler describes the South African empire-builder Cecil Rhodes as 'the first man of a new age' (p. 28) in which the West has begun its irrevocable descent towards what we would now call a heritage-dominated, museum culture. Wells takes the more conventional view of empires as the territorial manifestation of political power, but he goes beyond this since for him every failed empire is a flawed embodiment of the human striving to construct a global, and eventually a cosmic, order. As his idealistic explorer Cavor tells the Grand Lunar in *The First Men in the Moon*, ' "Our States and Empires are still the rawest sketches of what order will some day be" ' (Ch. 25). The notion of a galactic empire as the summit of

1 Isaac Asimov, *Foundation* (London: Weidenfeld & Nicolson, 1953). See especially Part II, ch. 7.

2 Richard D. Mullen, 'Blish, van Vogt, and the Uses of Spengler', *Riverside Quarterly* III:3 (August 1968), p. 172.

3 Oswald Spengler, *The Decline of the West*, trans. Charles Francis Atkinson (New York: Modern Library, 1962), pp. 13–14. Subsequent page references in text.

human achievement is implied at the end of *The War of the Worlds*, where the narrator envisages a successful struggle with the Martians for the control of Venus leading to a vision of human life 'spreading slowly from this little seed-bed of the solar system throughout the inanimate vastness of sidereal space' (II, 10).

II

What were the sources of Wells's ideas of imperialism? Born in 1866, he grew up at the height of late nineteenth-century imperial expansion—in 1877, for example, when he was eleven, Queen Victoria was proclaimed Empress of India. But he did not subscribe to the conventional British imperialism of Kipling or W. E. Henley, and (apart from *The Island of Doctor Moreau* and some short stories using tropical colonial settings) his early fiction usually reminds us less of an imperialist than of what Joseph Chamberlain, in a speech made in 1896, called a Little Englander.[4] *The Wonderful Visit*, *The Wheels of Chance*, *The Invisible Man* and *The War of the Worlds* are all steeped in the topography and social circumstances of the rural Home Counties. When an out-and-out imperialist appears in a Wells novel, the chances are that, like the aviation pioneer Butteridge in *The War in the Air*, he will be both a crook and a figure of fun. The little Englishman who is the hero of *The War in the Air*, Bert Smallways, is also a figure of fun when he tries to take the cares of the British Empire on his shoulders. ' "All this danger to the Empire worries me something frightful" ', complains Bert to his sister-in-law (1, vi).

Wells's political attitude to the Empire was made clear in his discussions with prominent Edwardian imperialists in the Coefficients Club, as reported in his *Autobiography*: 'The British Empire, I said, had to be the precursor of a world-state or nothing'. Wells clung for a time to the belief that 'the English-speaking community might play the part of leader and mediator towards a world commonweal' (II, p. 762). His principal model for understanding the role of empires in history was not contemporary Britain but ancient Rome. We know that he must have re-read Gibbon's *Decline and Fall of the Roman Empire* during the First World War when he began writing his own world-historical outline, but we do not know for certain when he first read it. He was introduced to the thought of the Enlighten-

4 Cf. Richard Brown, 'Little England: On Triviality in the Naive Comic Fictions of H. G. Wells', *Cahiers Victoriens et Edouardiens* 30 (October 1989), pp. 55–66.

ment in general during his adolescence, when he frequented the library at Uppark, the country house where his mother was house-keeper. This library had been collected by the freethinker Sir Harry Fetherstonehaugh, and in it, Wells recalls in his *Autobiography*, he read Plato's *Republic*, Swift, Voltaire, Tom Paine and Samuel John-son. Though it is not mentioned in the *Autobiography*, his fictional *alter ego* George Ponderevo in *Tono-Bungay* boasts that in the library at Bladesover House during his adolescence he read, 'with some reference now and then to the Atlas, Gibbon—in twelve volumes' (I, 1, v).

In *The Outline of History* Wells quotes extensively from Gibbon's *Decline and Fall*, and refers to him far more frequently than to any other historian apart from Herodotus. In a work ending with a visionary plea for global unity and world government, he turns repeatedly to Gibbon because the Roman Empire is the paradigm for all subsequent attempts at establishing imperial hegemony. 'The plot of the play', he wrote of universal history, 'is the long struggle through the Middle Ages and to our own time of the idea of the Roman Empire to adapt and re-establish itself as a form of universal human co-operation'.[5] Time and again these revivals of the Roman idea had relapsed into militarism and Caesarism, or autocratic dictatorship, on the later Roman pattern. Yet Wells also differs very explicitly from Gibbon in his view of the nature of Roman imperial-ism and the causes of its decline. Above all, he rejects Gibbon's rather complacent assurances that modern Europe was in no danger of sharing the fate of ancient Rome.

III

The Decline and Fall of the Roman Empire begins with what Wells in the *Outline of History* calls a 'prelude of splendour and tranquillity', a 'sunny review' of the age of the Antonines (p. 260). This view of Roman prosperity at its height is qualified with shafts of Gibbonian irony. For Wells in the *Outline*, however, Gibbon's irony was not sufficiently far-reaching, since his view of the second century AD was of a 'world of fine gentlemen upon the eighteenth-century model', rather than of a 'crude and gross plutocracy' (p. 447). The mass of human beings under the Roman Empire at its height were condemned to an acutely miserable existence, according to Wells.

5 H. G. Wells, 'History is One', in *The Atlantic Edition of the Works of H. G. Wells*, xxvii, p. 12.

Their lives lacked freedom and variety 'to a degree that a modern mind can scarcely imagine' (p. 263). The Empire was thus unable to command the ideological loyalty of its subjects. The cause of its collapse was not the successive waves of barbarian attacks, but the lack of an educated populace bound together by common political ideas. Gibbon, in his 'General Observations on the Fall of the Roman Empire in the West', argued that Europe was now secure from barbarian incursions thanks to the technology of modern warfare. 'Cannon and fortifications now form an impregnable barrier against the Tartar horse', he wrote, 'and Europe is secure from any future irruption of barbarians, since, before they can conquer, they must cease to be barbarous'.[6] Since there was no danger of civilised peoples relapsing into their original state, the wealth and happiness of humanity, with Europe in the vanguard, were assured.

To Wells, though he shared Gibbon's aspirations, this outlook was absurdly short-sighted. Gibbon and his Enlightenment contemporaries had remained blissfully unaware of the forces of political and social disintegration at work in their own time. With the coming of the Industrial Revolution, the 'new barbarism' was to be found not on the borders of Europe but 'within an easy walk perhaps' of the comfortable homes of Gibbon's refined and educated readers.[7] The argument that the Roman Empire had collapsed from its internal contradictions was not, of course, original to Wells. He may have absorbed it from a number of sources in the socialist movement, including a book that he had certainly read at Uppark during his adolescence, *Progress and Poverty* (1880) by the American socialist and land-tax campaigner Henry George.[8] George begins with strictly economic arguments but ends with a broadly speculative discussion of 'The Law of Human Progress', which must have appealed strongly to Wells. Here he attributes the collapse of the great civilisations of the past to their unequal distribution of power and wealth. Repeatedly, he points to the fall of Rome as a terrible example of the doom which could overtake a non-socialist America. George argues, in terms that Wells would later echo, that 'The barbarism which

6 Edward Gibbon, *The Decline and Fall of the Roman Empire*, ed. Dero T. Saunders (London: Penguin, 1981), p. 628. Subsequent page references in text.

7 H. G. Wells, *The Outline of History*, pp. 452–53.

8 On Henry George see H. G. Wells, *Experiment in Autobiography*, I, pp. 177–79.

overwhelmed Rome came not from without, but from within'.[9] The future of nineteenth-century society is equally precarious, and George criticises Gibbon for the complacency that led him to believe that modern civilisation could never be destroyed. In George's words, 'The civilised world is trembling on the verge of a great movement. Either it must be a leap upward, which will open the way to advances yet undreamed of, or it must be a plunge downward, which will carry us back toward barbarism' (p. 385).

Very similar ideas are to be found not only in Wells's later writings in historiography and social criticism, but in his early science fiction, as we have already seen. When he met President Theodore Roosevelt in 1906, the President took him to task over the imaginary future outlined in *The Time Machine*. Roosevelt refused to believe in Wells's forecast of the division of the human race into degenerate subterranean workers on the one hand, and decadent and powerless property-owners on the other.[10] He was a convinced individualist, but presumably had some acquaintance with American socialist thought.[11] Through this conversation we can glimpse the influence on *The Time Machine* of Henry George, with his view that the 'natural monopoly which is given by the possession of land' is the major cause of inequality (*Progress and Poverty*, p. 366). George showed how this monopoly led in time to social decay and, ultimately, collapse. This is where his words most clearly anticipate the society of Eloi and Morlocks in *The Time Machine*:

> The earth is the tomb of dead empires, no less than dead men. Instead of progress fitting men for greater progress, every civilisation that was in its own time as vigorous and advancing as ours is now, has of itself come to a stop. Over and over again, art has declined, learning sunk, power waned, population become sparse, until the people who had built great temples and mighty cities [. . . ,] cultivated the earth like a garden and introduced the utmost refinement into the minute affairs of life, remained but a remnant of squalid barbarians, who had lost even the memory of what their ancestors had done, and regarded the surviving frag-

9 Henry George, *Progress and Poverty* (London: Dent, 1911), p. 369. Subsequent page references in text.

10 H. G. Wells, *The Future in America*, p. 349.

11 See H. G. Wells, *Experiment in Autobiography*, II, p. 756.

ments of their grandeur as the work of genii, or of the mighty race before the flood. (p. 343)

Not only does this passage seem a very exact description of the world of the Eloi, whom Wells was to portray living in a pastoral setting amid their ruined palaces and temples like a race bereft of energy, foresight and cultural memory; but when George goes on to say that such a decayed civilisation is invariably supplanted by a 'fresh race coming from a lower level' (p. 343), we have the image of the Morlocks emerging from their underground tunnels.

IV

It can hardly be a coincidence that, on his first journey abroad, Wells headed straight for the ruins of Rome. He and Jane left their home in Surrey on 7 March 1898, and arrived in Rome by train the following evening. Next morning, accompanied by their friend George Gissing, they enjoyed the first of many rambles through the city, where they stayed for five weeks. They were frequent visitors to the Forum— sadly, Gissing noted, fenced off with iron railings[12]—as well as to the Palatine Hill and the other remnants of the ancient city.[13] Gissing, who was their constant companion, spoke often of his plans for *Veranilda*, the historical romance of sixth-century Rome that he was busily researching. The writing of *Veranilda* did not proceed smoothly, however, and the unfinished novel eventually came out posthumously in 1904. Wells's preface, which had been commissioned for the volume, was rejected by Gissing's executors and had to be published separately.[14] Few of Gissing's admirers have had a good word to say for *Veranilda*, and a curious feature of Wells's preface is that the part of the novel he evokes most eloquently is the part that its author did not live to write. In a letter to Gissing in January 1898,

12 H. G. Wells, undated letter to Harry Quilter from Hotel Alibert, Rome. MS. Special Collections, Hofstra University.

13 According to Jane Wells's pocket diary for 1898 (MS. Wells Collection, University of Illinois) they went three times to the Colosseum and twice to the Forum and the Palatine Hill. See also Patrick Parrinder, 'The Roman Spring of George Gissing and H. G. Wells', *Gissing Newsletter* xxi:3 (July 1985), pp. 1–12.

14 H. G. Wells, 'George Gissing: An Impression', reprinted in Royal A. Gettmann, ed., *George Gissing and H.G. Wells: Their Friendship and Correspondence* (London: Hart-Davis, 1961), pp. 260–77. Subsequent page references in text.

Wells had referred to *Veranilda* as 'that story of the sunset and the coming of the wild men again'.[15] His account of the book's unwritten conclusion is in the same spirit:

> the main threads run clear to their end; in a moment the tumult of the assailing Goths, terrible by reason of their massacre at Tibur, would have become audible, and the wave of panic that left Rome to the dogs and vermin have swept us to the end. And the end was morning, a sunlit silence upon the empty Forum, upon the as yet unruined Palatine Hill, upon the yet unshattered Basilica of Constantine. For just that one tremendous moment in her history Rome lay still. (pp. 275–76)

Here Gissing's somewhat decorous historical romance is seen through the eyes of the author of *The War of the Worlds* and *The Time Machine*; but the passage also reveals the Gibbonian sensibility that Wells brought to bear on the spectacle of ancient Rome. In the second century, according to Gibbon, 'the empire of Rome comprehended the fairest part of the earth and the most civilised portion of mankind' (p. 27). Its fall was 'the most awful scene in the history of mankind' (p. 690). Gibbon's great history ends in the fifteenth century with a description of the ruins of Rome left by two servants of Pope Eugenius IV. These two men ascended the Capitoline Hill and agreed that, 'in proportion to her former greatness, the fall of Rome was the more awful and deplorable. . . . "Cast your eyes upon the Palatine hill and seek among the shapeless and enormous fragments the marble theatre, the obelisks, the colossal statues, the porticoes of Nero's palace; survey the other hills of the city, [and] the vacant space is interrupted only by ruins and gardens" ' (pp. 685–86). Such a prospect of colossal statues, obelisks, ruins and gardens had been described by Wells before he either visited Rome itself or met George Gissing.

Mary Shelley's Last Man, Lionel Verney, finally fetches up in the city of monuments, Rome, in which his last act will be to leave a monument to himself—presumably the novel that bears his name. Wells's science fiction transfers the scene of imperial collapse from Rome to the 'Dead London' of *The War of the Worlds* and the

Richmond of *The Time Machine*.[16] The Arcadian classicism of the world of the Eloi and Morlocks is the most singular feature of a landscape supposedly set eight hundred thousand years in the future. The survival of classical architectural forms and ornamental designs such as the carved griffins' heads and the ' "suggestions of old Phœnician decorations" ' (§4) cannot be plausibly explained at this distance of time. Moreover, the Eloi, clad in ' "sandals or buskins" ' and purple tunics (§3), match the landscape in which they move. No likely degree of cultural continuity, or of deliberate historical revivalism at some future date, could account for this. The conclusion to be drawn (already hinted at in Chapter Three above) is that there appear to be two timescales superimposed on one another in *The Time Machine*. Each is internally consistent, and Wells shows great subtlety and dexterity in silently switching from one to the other.

Since all the surviving monuments from previous ages in the year 802,701 are described in a state of ruin and decay, we do not reflect that in some cases, however much the durability of building materials and storage techniques has improved, the decay ought to have gone very much further. The Palace of Green Porcelain exemplifies this. Inside its long-neglected display cases, the Time Traveller finds a box of matches and a perfectly preserved lump of camphor. The implausibility of this find is so great that Wells must have realised that he had to meet the reader's incredulity halfway:

> 'In the universal decay this volatile substance had chanced to survive, perhaps through many thousands of centuries. It reminded me of a sepia painting I had once seen done from the ink of a fossil Belemnite that must have perished and become fossilised millions of years ago.' (§8)

Just as the ink of the Belemnite was still usable, the camphor burns well enough to start a bonfire which turns into a blazing inferno.

The Palace of Green Porcelain, the most elaborate of the buildings that have lingered on into the age of the Eloi and Morlocks, is a consummate symbol of the human continuity that has finally been

16 Robert Crossley develops the parallel between *The Last Man* and *The Time Machine* in 'In the Palace of Green Porcelain: Artifacts from the Museums of Science Fiction', in Tom Shippey, ed., *Fictional Space: Essays on Contemporary Science Fiction* (Oxford: Blackwell, 1991), p. 86. See also Patrick Parrinder, 'From Mary Shelley to *The War of the Worlds*'.

broken. This ' "ancient monument of an intellectual age" ' (?8) has been well described by Robert Crossley as a '*memento mori* for the human species'.[17] Yet the age to which it is a monument is, pre-eminently, the nineteenth century. Its survival suggests that the future civilisations intervening between our own time and 802,701 have scarcely developed at all beyond the technology and culture with which the Time Traveller was already familiar. The museum as an institution apparently continued to hold the same key position, and to fulfil the same function, as it did in the age of Queen Victoria (which suggests, among other things, that the Traveller's own invention of a time machine had not been exploited by any succeeding civilisation). The layout of the Palace of Green Porcelain, with its library and galleries of natural history, mineralogy, palaeontology, ethnography, technical chemistry, industrial machinery and armaments is precisely what a late Victorian visitor might have expected. No wonder the Traveller describes it as a ' "latter-day South Kensington!" ' (§8). Its state of preservation in the future compares very favourably with that of a neglected classical temple or medieval abbey in our own day, especially as its ruins, unlike theirs, have not been pillaged. Evidently the Time Traveller was the first being who ever thought to look there for matches and camphor.

The Palace of Green Porcelain, then, belongs to the foreshortened, historical scale of future time—as it were, to AD 2701 rather than 802,701. Yet the Eloi and Morlocks could only emerge within the long perspective of evolutionary time. The Traveller's influential theory of the emergence of the Eloi and Morlocks as a result of the class divisions observable in the nineteenth-century city fits the shorter rather than the longer timescale, however. The class struggle may be (as Marxists would argue) the motor of history, but to project it as the factor bringing about a permanent species differentiation is another matter. Implicitly, the level at which *The Time Machine* operates as a social fable about class conflict appeals to historical rather than biological reasoning.

As he discovers the true state of the Eloi, the Time Traveller fleetingly experiences a ' "Carlyle-like scorn of this wretched aristocracy-in-decay" ' (§7). He imagines that they must initially have declined into a state of 'mere beautiful futility" ', ' "like the Carlovingian kings" ' (§7). The first reference is presumably to Carlyle's denunciation of the 'Idle Aristocracy, the Owners of the

17 Robert Crossley, 'In the Palace of Green Porcelain', p. 86.

Soil of England' in *Past and Present*,[18] while the second seems to be an allusion to Gibbon.[19] As the Traveller learns more of the Morlocks, however, he comes to replace this partly historical explanation of the connection between the two species with a biological one. Reluctantly, he has to concede that the Eloi and Morlocks are locked into a symbiotic relationship of predators and prey, like men and domestic animals. Of the three animal species to which the Morlocks are explicitly compared—apes or lemurs, rats, and ants—the description of the Morlocks as ' "ant-like" ' (§7) has wider resonances in Wells's science fiction, and reintroduces the theme of the fall of empires.

V

Within the world of 802,701 the Time Traveller is engaged in a desperate struggle with the Morlocks for mastery. Wells later wrote a short story called 'The Empire of the Ants' (1905), in which colonial settlers in the upper Amazon are shown fleeing before a new race of super-intelligent ants. The story's narrator concludes that there is nothing to stop the ants from 'dispossess[ing] man over the whole of tropical south America'. 'By 1920 they will be half-way down the Amazon', he forecasts. 'I fix 1950 or '60 at the latest for the discovery of Europe'.[20] 'The Empire of the Ants' is a literal projection of the vision of warfare between species which, elsewhere, Wells presents in metaphorical form. The essence of the power-relationship between human beings and ants is that, for Wells, it is reversible. On several occasions when he compares humankind to ants, he does so to demonstrate how easily we could be controlled and destroyed by a superior species. In *The War of the Worlds*, he portrays the Martian invasion of England as an experience of colonisation in reverse: as the Martians are to Europeans, so the Europeans are to the natives of Tasmania, who were wiped out after a 'war of extermination waged by European immigrants' (I, 1). In the novel's opening paragraph the complacency of human beings, 'serene in their assurance of their empire over matter', is compared to that of creatures even smaller

18 Thomas Carlyle, *Past and Present* (London: Chapman and Hall, 1889), p. 153.

19 Compare Edward Gibbon's account of the 'dregs of the Carlovingian race' in *The History of the Decline and Fall of the Roman Empire*, ed. J. B. Bury (London: Methuen, 1898), v, p. 292.

20 H. G. Wells' 'The Empire of the Ants', in *Complete Short Stories* (London: Benn, 1927), p. 108.

than ants: bacteria, or the 'infusoria under the microscope' (I, 1).
When it seems that the Martians have utterly defeated their oppo-
nents, the narrator meets the Artilleryman who gives voice to a
useless defiance: ' "This isn't a war," ' he says, " ' . . . any more
than there's war between men and ants" ' (II, 7). But soon after that
it is the Martian empire on earth that collapses, undermined by the
very bacteria that had earlier been invoked as the representatives of
life in its humblest form. At the end of the novel the narrator
wanders through the deserted and partly ruined streets of London
until he comes upon the ruins of the Martian invaders themselves.

The theme of men versus ants is picked up again in later romances
such as *The War in the Air*, where New York is destroyed early in the
twentieth century by bombardment from German airships. ' "We're
just ants in ant-hill cities" ' says the disillusioned German Lieuten-
ant Kurt: ' "New York was nothing but an ant-hill kicked to pieces
by a fool!" ' (7, vii). Between *The War of the Worlds* and *The War in the
Air*, Wells had nevertheless produced an astonishing tribute to the
social cohesion and powers of collective organisation attributable to
ants and ant-hill cities: this was the world of the Selenites, or
'ant-men' as they are called (Ch. 22), in *The First Men in the Moon*.
Wells's explorer Cavor is abandoned on the moon by Bedford, but
manages to send back to earth his observations of the Selenites in a
series of radio messages. Bedford, who intercepts these messages
once he has returned to earth, develops the comparison with ants at
considerable length. 'The moon is, indeed, a sort of vast ant-hill', he
concludes, 'only, instead of there being only four or five sorts of ant,
there are many hundred different sorts of Selenite, and almost every
gradation between one sort and another' (Ch. 24).

A colony or empire of ants is a society based on functional
inequality. The class division between queens and worker ants would,
if transferred to human society, threaten the survival of the communal organisation—or so Wells and Henry George were arguing in
their analysis of the fall of empires. In creating the Selenites,
however, Wells used the analogy of the ant to show how a stable
imperium could be based on functional inequality, so long as it
consisted of alien creatures innocent of all human ideas of freedom
and dignity. The Selenites are, for the most part, slaves subjected to
the highest possible degree of physical and mental control and
manipulation. Those chosen to converse with Cavor are, however,
privileged individuals granted a certain degree of intellectual licence.
At the summit of Selenite society, occupying the position of the

queen ant, is the grotesque figure of the Grand Lunar whose interrogation of Cavor is reminiscent of Gulliver's interview with the King of Brobdingnag.

The Selenites are not merely metaphorical ants, since their life underground in the 'lunar caves' (Ch. 22) is a far more elaborate version of the subterranean society of the Morlocks. The Selenites have created a grandiose underground architecture, so that the chamber of the Grand Lunar is approached by a series of halls linked by staircases which Cavor compares to the steps of Santa Maria in Aracoeli at Rome (Ch. 25), a church that Wells and Jane had visited on 27 March 1898.[21] Cavor has great difficulty in making the Grand Lunar understand terrestrial architecture, particularly as he reveals that the earliest men had begun by living in caves. Why should humans 'build houses when they might descend into excavations', the Grand Lunar wishes to know (Ch. 25)? Even more disconcerting to the ruler of the Selenites is the fact that human beings are disunited and have no Grand Earthly. Cavor unwisely takes the opportunity to boast of the Anglo-Saxon peoples' sturdy resistance to 'autocrats and emperors' (Ch. 25).

The First Men in the Moon begins with Bedford dreaming of building a commercial empire based on the anti-gravity substance Cavorite. Bedford's dream is of a vast capitalistic monopoly controlling everything; he tells Cavor, the inventor, that 'we might make wealth enough to work any sort of social revolution we fancied, we might own and order the whole world' (Ch. 1). The novel ends with the stable empire of the Selenites, in which decay or revolution seems impossible; and finally it seems that the intrusion of the barbarians, Cavor and Bedford, has been ruthlessly suppressed. The satirical ambiguity of *The First Men in the Moon* is evident from the fact that both Bedford's commercial fantasy and the ant-hill state of the Selenites approximate to the world government of which Wells himself dreamed—yet they are also deeply and intentionally repugnant. The underground architecture of the Selenites' ant-hill society resembles that of the Morlocks in that it signifies both civilised development and subterranean barbarity; yet it is worth remembering that in his cinematic epic of the future produced in the 1930s, *Things to Come*, Wells imagined the construction of a utopian city underground.

21 Jane Wells's pocket diary for 1898, MS. Wells Collection, University of Illinois.

VI

There is a slightly later Wellsian romance which deals directly with the fall of empires and alludes unmistakably to Gibbon's epic of the decline and fall of Rome. This is *The War in the Air*, published in 1908 at the height of the arms race between the great powers which was to lead to the First World War. *The War in the Air* is set in the very near future, in a world of bicycles, ballooning, airships and monorails. Wells's principal aim in what he later called a 'fantasy of possibility'[22] was to link his intimations of the collapse of modern civilisation to the imminent development of aerial warfare.

His hero Bert Smallways grows up in an atmosphere of virulent popular imperialism, summed up in the figure of Butteridge, the aviation pioneer who proclaims himself an 'Imperial Englishman' at every opportunity. (It soon appears, however, that he is on the point of selling his technical secrets to the Germans.) Swept off inadvertently in Butteridge's balloon, Bert Smallways is blown across the Channel to Germany, where he encounters the 'central figure of the world drama', Prince Karl Albert, 'the darling of the Imperialist spirit' who is compared by his followers to Alexander and the young Caesar (4,i). The Prince's expedition across the Atlantic with his war fleet to bomb the United States is even more disastrous than Napoleon's march on Moscow. The air fleets of all the great powers take part in the conflagration, and no sooner has battle been joined between the Germans and the Americans than the Asiatic powers send their airships across the Pacific to attack the German base at Niagara Falls. In Chapters 10 and 11—'The World Under the War' and 'The Great Collapse'—Wells draws the lessons of his fantasy for the fate of modern civilisation. First he compares the early twentieth century, as Gibbon had compared the middle of the eighteenth century, to the Roman empire at its height in the age of the Antonines. Then he draws the moral of civilisation's swift collapse.

According to Wells's narrator, it was inherent in the nature of modern society itself that Gibbon's multi-volume epic could be superseded by a brief science-fiction thriller. Under the war in the air, 'The world passed at a stride from a unity and simplicity broader than that of the Roman Empire at its best, to a social fragmentation as complete as the robber-baron period of the Middle Ages' (9, iii). 'In five short years the world and the scope of human life have

22 H. G. Wells, Preface, dated 'Easton Glebe, Dunmow, 1921', to *The Sleeper Awakes and Men Like Gods* (London: Odham's, n.d.).

undergone a retrogressive change as great as that between the age of the Antonines and the Europe of the ninth century' (9, iii).To ask whether mankind could have prevented the disaster would be as idle as to ask whether the Romans could have prevented the 'slow decline and fall, the gradual social disorganization . . . that closed the chapter of the Empire of the West' (9, i). In these self-consciously Gibbonian passages Wells is not only forecasting the collapse of modern civilisation and a return to barbarism, the coming of a new dark age. He is also putting forward prophetic science fiction as a new form of historiography, as suited to its times as Gibbon's encyclo-paedic work was to the serenely complacent eighteenth century.

CHAPTER SIX

New Worlds for Old:
The Prophet at Large

I

The War in the Air is the first of Wells's globetrotting novels. After his balloon flight to Germany, Bert Smallways is transported across the Atlantic as a stowaway with the Kaiser's Zeppelin fleet. He witnesses the aerial siege of New York and the battle of Niagara Falls. All the time he has with him the secret plans for the Butteridge flying-machine, which he acquired in the confusion which led to his being swept off in a balloon from Dymchurch beach. Eventually, Bert personally delivers the plans to the President of the United States. By the time that he wrote this novel Wells, too, was a Kentish boy who had met the US President. Later he was to become the prototype of the modern politically-conscious international writer, a journalist and public figure on the world stage who had high-minded conversations with Lenin, Stalin and Franklin Roosevelt. He was elected international president of PEN (Poets, Essayists, Novelists), an organisation of which he was a co-founder, in 1934. In the same year, some of his admirers banded together to form the first H. G. Wells Society. They debated whether to change its name to the Open Conspiracy after Wells's book of 1928 advocating a popular movement for world government, but in the end they decided to call it Cosmopolis.[1]

Wells's son Anthony West has claimed that between the wars his father did 'as much as any man then living to create the climate of opinion in the middle ground that was to make the creation of the United Nations and the establishment of the European Economic Community . . . inevitable'.[2] Many others have seen him as a failed

---

1 See David C. Smith, *H. G. Wells: Desperately Mortal*, p. 333. Earlier, in 1907, groups of Wells's followers had formed the 'Samurai Societies' named after the ruling élite of *A Modern Utopia*. See Smith, op. cit., p. 101.

2 Anthony West, *H. G. Wells: Aspects of a Life* (London: Hutchinson, 1984), p. 132.

prophet of world order, and there are those who would relegate his visions of global and cosmic integration to the storehouse of discredited collectivist fantasies. Nevertheless, despite constant setbacks, the Wellsian ideal of world citizenship has gained ground throughout the twentieth century. In the 1930s he wrote that 'I am English by origin but I am an early World-Man and I live in exile from the community of my desires'.[3] All three parts of this statement—his English origins, his cosmopolitan outlook, and his sense of exile from a longed-for new world—will be explored in this chapter.

In labelling himself an 'early World-Man', he was, as so often, using a biological and anthropological metaphor to express the crisis of modern political identity. *Homo sapiens*, the World-Man, was struggling to evolve out of the divided humanity of the era of sovereign nation-states. Only by developing into World-Men could humankind survive the modern industrial age in which, for the first time, the species was capable of bringing about its own extinction. Wells's ideal of world government was first conceived at the zenith of European imperialism, and in some respects he was preaching a kind of super-imperialism which remained rooted in imperial ideology. Though an outspoken critic of conventional empires, he looked to a new civilisation unified by its attachment to Western rationality, with a centralised government run by a scientific élite and combining moral authority with military strength.

It so happens that the years 1880–1920, during which nearly all of his major works were written, were not only the heyday of competitive world-conquest but a period of resurgent cultural nationalism in England itself.[4] Wells had little or no sympathy with Chamberlain's 'Little Englanders', but his English origins are unmistakable and his early writing did much to fix a certain image of ordinary English life in his reader's minds. His Englishness is part and parcel of his wider outlook. He may be classed as a 'provincial' writer in more than one sense of the term. No doubt there is something to be said for his attempts to construct a religion of humanity without Comte and a socialism without Marx, but his hostility to these two thinkers partly reflects his sense that their methodical, system-building habits were

---

3 H. G. Wells, *H. G. Wells in Love*, ed. G. P. Wells (London: Faber & Faber, 1984), p. 235.

4 See Robert Colls and Philip Dodd, eds., *Englishness: Politics and Culture 1880–1920* (London: Croom Helm, 1986), passim.

alien to the pragmatic English mind.[5] On a more positive note, he is provincial in that he grew up on the underside of the British class system, the son of a small shopkeeper and a lady's maid, and his early life was spent in the small towns and villages of south-east England. He was not a Londoner by birth or upbringing, and it was thanks to the newly-instituted scheme of government scholarships for teacher-training that, at the age of eighteen, he moved to the metropolis. He was later to recreate the scenes of his Home Counties childhood with a mixture of warmth and biting sarcasm in novels such as *The Invisible Man* and *The History of Mr Polly*, written just as the new rural ideal of southern English life—to be seen slightly later in the Georgian poets—was taking shape.

No sooner has he imagined a rural idyll than he sets out to disrupt it—as both *The Invisible Man* and *Mr Polly* bear witness. Wells's own father 'grew up to gardening and cricket [he played for Kent], and remained an out-of-doors, open-air man to the day of his death'[6]— and what could be more provincial and English than that? Yet Wells seems to have inherited his restlessness from his father who (as his son recalled in *The Future in America*) 'still possesses the stout oak box that he had made to emigrate withal, everything was arranged that would have got me and my brothers born across the ocean, and only the coincidence of a business opportunity and an illness of my mother's, arrested that' (pp. 24–25). Joseph Wells had tried and failed to break free from the routine of life in the Home Counties. His son was luckier and more successful. As George Ponderevo says in *Tono-Bungay*, 'One gets hit by some unusual transverse force, one is jerked out of one's stratum and lives crosswise for the rest of the time, and, as it were, in a succession of samples. That has been my lot' (I, 1, i). George reaches the heights of London society as a result of his uncle's runaway success with a patent-medicine business, but at the end of the novel, like Joseph Wells, he seems to be looking away from Europe towards the New World. He has become a naval architect whose pet project (a destroyer) 'isn't intended for the Empire, or indeed for the hands of any European power'. 'I have come to see myself from the outside, my country from the outside—without illusions', George adds (IV, 3, iv). That was certainly Wells's aim.

5 On Comte, see H. G. Wells, 'The So-Called Science of Sociology', in *An Englishman Looks at the World* (London: Cassell, 1914), pp. 192–93. On Marx, see *Experiment in Autobiography*, I, pp. 263–64.

6 H. G. Wells, *Experiment in Autobiography*, I, p. 54.

It would seem that, metaphorically and to some extent literally, the New World was the necessary foil to the bankrupt Old World in Wells's writing. In a 1915 study of *The World of H. G. Wells* which was much the best critical study written on its subject during his lifetime, Van Wyck Brooks claimed that there was a natural affinity between Wells and his American readers. 'His mind', Brooks observed, 'is a disinherited mind, not connected with tradition, thinking and acting *de novo* because there is nothing to prevent it from doing so'.[7] Wells's sense of disinheritance may doubtless be attributed to his insecure childhood (the family broke up when he was thirteen) and to his illness as a young adult; but such experiences are common enough. One frequent recourse of the disinherited is an aggressive, chauvinistic identification with the aims of a particular group or society, giving rise to some of the ugliest manifestations of modern nationalism. Wells's identification, instead, was with the global aims of socialism and science. It was likely, also, as a 'disinherited' writer, that he would veer between autobiographical fiction and outright fantasy; his was too restless an imagination to stay for long in secure possession of a clearly defined social world, as Jane Austen and Anthony Trollope had done. In later life he took such opportunities as came his way to travel the world, and for a time he maintained a house in France. These experiences were to be reflected in the widening horizons of his autobiographical novels, but they only sharpened his sense of the global need for reconstruction and change. He remained in exile from the community of his desires.

II

In both fictional and non-fictional forms, Wellsian autobiography follows the conventional shape of the *Bildungsroman*, in which the hero progresses from narrow origins to a position reflecting the author's general view of human life. Wells's protagonists may be divided into those who share his mature authorial consciousness (reflected in the title of the triumphal final chapter of his *Experiment in Autobiography*, 'The Idea of a Planned World'), and those who do not. The latter—comic heroes or anti-heroes such as Kipps, Bert Smallways, and Mr Polly—remain limited, provincial and English. Art Kipps, an orphan growing up in New Romney in Kent, finds his first home in the backyard and kitchen of his uncle's shop in the

7 Van Wyck Brooks, *The World of H. G. Wells* (London: Unwin, 1915), p. 178. Subsequent page references in text.

High Street, and especially in the corner under the ironing-board where, with the aid of an old shawl, he makes a cubby-house. This 'served him for several years as the indisputable hub of the world' (I, 1, i). The wider horizons opened up for him as a young man by a timely legacy leave no lasting impression, and finally we see the mature Kipps happily ensconced in another small High Street shop, this time in Hythe (which is only a few miles from New Romney). Alfred Polly, too, begins in obscurity and ends in a similar though more contented state at the Potwell Inn, a deeply rural (and highly unlikely) English Rabelaisian paradise. Bert Smallways also remains a Kentish shop-boy at heart. The President of the United States helps him to get back to England, where he is reunited with his Edna and settles down in his home town of Bun Hill; meanwhile, industrial civilisation is destroyed by war and plague. In *The Outline of History* Wells described human life as a 'race between education and catastrophe' (p. 608), and in Kipps, Polly and Smallways he outlined the comedy of stubbornly uneducated lives, not World-Men but little Englishmen, who could take no part in that race.

Kipps and Polly had been sent to dingy private schools. In *The History of Mr Polly*, Wells uses a memorable image to indicate what a proper imperial education might have done for his hero:

> I remember seeing a picture of Education—in some place. I think it was Education, but quite conceivably it represented the Empire teaching her Sons, and I have a strong impression that it was a wall painting upon some public building in Manchester or Birmingham or Glasgow, but very possibly I am mistaken about that. It represented a glorious woman, with a wise and fearless face, stooping over her children, and pointing them to far horizons. The sky displayed the pearly warmth of a summer dawn, and all the painting was marvellously bright as if with the youth and hope of the delicately beautiful children in the foreground. She was telling them, one felt, of the great prospect of life that opened before them, of the splendours of sea and mountain they might travel and see, the joys of skill they might acquire, and the pride of effort, and the devotions and nobilities it was theirs to achieve. . . . She was reminding them of their great heritage as English children, rulers of more than one-fifth of mankind, of the obligation to do and be the best that such a pride of empire entails, of their

essential nobility and knighthood, and of the restraints and charities and disciplined strength that is becoming in knights and rulers. . . .

The education of Mr Polly did not follow this picture very closely (1, ii).

The picture of Education belongs in the bombastic tradition of Victorian political allegory. Wells's mockery distances him from the representation of the 'pride of empire', though the passage certainly draws on the romantic allure of imperialist mythology. Characteristically, he would channel such feelings in the direction of cosmopolitan idealism. In *The Outline of History*, there is an illustration by J. F. Horrabin showing Britannia, Germania, Marianne and other 'Tribal Gods—*national symbols for which men would die*—of the Nineteenth Century' (p. 529). Nevertheless, in the *Autobiography* Wells attributes his childish sexual awakening to his 'naive, direct admiration for the lovely bodies, as they seemed, of those political divinities of Tenniel's in *Punch*, and . . . the plaster casts of Greek statuary that adorned the Crystal Palace' (I, p. 80). The picture of Education stands somewhere between these figures and the representation, in Wells's *A Modern Utopia*, of a Utopian coin portraying not Britannia, as the old English penny piece did, but 'Peace, as a beautiful woman, reading with a child out of a great book, and behind them . . . stars, and an hour-glass, halfway-run' (p. 72). In *Mr Polly*, imperial Education is beckoning to the horizon at dawn rather than reading to her children at twilight, suggesting a stirring of energies in contrast to Utopian calm.

Just as the allegory of Peace excludes the adult male (normally associated with violence), the picture of imperial Education offers no position for the disinherited. In that respect, it is simply irrelevant to the needs of Alfred Polly, and remains no more than a dream for Wells himself. In his childhood he could not realistically aspire to 'nobility and knighthood', nor could he march toward the 'great prospect of life' in a straight line. Instead, disentanglement from the confined world of his upbringing came on Wells very suddenly. Van Wyck Brooks, no doubt influenced by George Ponderevo's reflections in *Tono-Bungay*, expressed this as follows:

> The world of shopkeeping in England is a world girt about with immemorial subjections; it is, one might say, a moss-covered world; and to shake oneself loose from it is to become a rolling stone, a drifting and unsettled, a detached

and acutely personal, individual. It is to pass from a certain confined social maturity, a confused mellowness, into a world wholly adventurous and critical, into a freedom which achieves itself at the expense of solidity and warmth.
(p. 134)

It is profoundly significant, in this light, that Wells launched his literary career not with autobiographical fiction (this was to come later) but by leaping with one bound from the familiar to the exotic, from the Home Counties to the 'wholly adventurous and critical' world of his short stories and scientific romances.

In many of the early stories the theme of escape is paramount, as the hero undergoes an 'out of the body' experience (extending, in 'Under the Knife', to a cosmic journey to the other end of the galaxy), or disrupts the frame of experience in some way (as in 'The Man Who Could Work Miracles', where Mr Fotheringay manages to stop the earth's rotation). The geography of imperialism is reflected in stories such as 'In the Avu Observatory' set in Borneo, 'The Treasure in the Forest' and *The Island of Doctor Moreau* in the South Pacific, 'Aepyornis Island' in the Caribbean, 'The Empire of the Ants' and 'The Country of the Blind' in South America, and 'The Pearl of Love' in ancient India, not to mention 'In the Abyss' on the ocean bed and 'The Crystal Egg' on Mars. In other stories the homely English setting is disrupted by strange events, which are often exotic in the strict sense. ' "New Genus, by Heavens! And in England!" ' exclaims the entomologist Hapley, confronted by the phantom of a strange moth in an airtight laboratory somewhere in Kent,[8] while another story, 'The Flowering of the Strange Orchid', takes place in a Home Counties greenhouse. The protagonist in 'The Remarkable Case of Davidson's Eyes' simultaneously experiences life in London and on Antipodes Island.

In his preface to *The Country of the Blind and Other Stories*, Wells looked back on the spontaneous and apparently irresponsible conception of his early stories: 'Little men in canoes upon sunlit oceans would come floating out of nothingness, . . . violent conflicts would break out amidst the flower-beds of suburban gardens; I would discover I was peering into remote and mysterious worlds ruled by an order logical indeed but other than our common sanity' (p. iv). The apparent interchangeability of the settings is very notable, but where the 'little men in canoes' were a staple of late Victorian

8 H. G. Wells, 'The Moth', in *Complete Short Stories*, p. 307.

adventure fiction, the violent conflicts in suburban gardens are typical of Wells's scientific romances. In *The War of the Worlds* the first Martians land at Woking in Surrey, where Wells was then living. The initial idea for the story came from his brother Frank. Wells, who had just learned to ride a bicycle, 'wheeled about the district marking down suitable places for destruction by my Martians'.[9] Today the sandpits on Horsell Common near Woking are still instantly recognisable to a reader of *The War of the Worlds*. Nevertheless, in the many media adaptations of the book its original setting has almost invariably been discarded; the local realism of the story, which works out triumphantly on the printed page, turns out to be highly adaptable. In Orson Welles's 1938 adaptation for CBS radio the Martians land in New Jersey, while in George Pal's 1953 movie version they attack Northern California. A mass panic comparable in scale to that aroused by the Orson Welles dramatisation has been reported from Ecuador, where in 1949 a 'localised version' of *The War of the Worlds* broadcast in Quito led to a riot in which the crowd stormed and set fire to the radio station.[10] Wells's tale had proved to be universal even if his chosen setting was highly particular.

The Wellsian scientific romance combines irresponsible and 'impatient' imagination with the disciplined working-out of the initial hypothesis. To that extent, it reflects the scientific ideal and may even run parallel to the processes of scientific explanation. When he dreamed of 'peering into remote and mysterious worlds', he was turning his scientific studies to imaginative account. In later years, however, he would claim that the 'central fact' of his student years was not his experience of empirical observation through the microscope but the 'complete and ordered view' of the universe he had gained from Huxley.[11] Such a hunger for the universal was at the heart of his notion of disciplined imagination, as is clear from a much-quoted exchange with Joseph Conrad that he records in his *Autobiography*. Lying on Sandgate beach, the two men debated the best way to describe a boat that they could see riding out in the water:

> it was all against Conrad's over-sensitized receptivity that a boat could ever be just a boat. He wanted to see it and to see

9 H. G. Wells, *Experiment in Autobiography*, II, p. 543.

10 See Michael Draper, 'The Martians in Ecuador', *Wellsian* ns5 (Summer 1982), pp. 35–36.

11 H. G. Wells, *A Modern Utopia*, p. 376.

it only in relation to something else—a story, a thesis. And I suppose if I had been pressed about it I would have betrayed a disposition to link that story or thesis to something still more extensive and that to something still more extensive and so ultimately to link it up to my philosophy and my world outlook. (II, p. 619)

For Wells it is not just a boat but a specimen, a model—as likely as not, a model of social experience and social relations. Both his science fiction and his social fiction rely on different kinds of model-building.

In science fiction, the best example of Wellsian model-building is 'The Man of the Year Million', originally proposed in a fanciful short story, but later overtly incorporated into *The War of the Worlds* and covertly into *The Time Machine* and *The First Men in the Moon*. The man of the year million consisted of little else but a hand and an enormous brain. All other physical organs had atrophied, since they were no longer needed. The Martians and the Grand Lunar are realisations of this idea of the future man, while the Eloi and Morlocks are the products of physical evolution in a reverse direction once humanity has failed to evolve into a higher being. After 1901 Wells abandoned such fictions with their allegorical glimpses of the far future, turning to realistic and comic fiction in which characters such as Kipps and Polly are often held up as sociological models or specimens. In *Tono-Bungay* the social analysis is held together by Wells's modelling vision of Bladesover, the country-house on the chalk downs, as a 'complete authentic microcosm' (I, 1, iii) of traditional English society. George Ponderevo's understanding of this world is conditioned by his upbringing in the servants' quarters of the great house. His later escapades, which include a buccaneering mission to tropical Africa, only confirm his hunch that England and its Empire are permeated by the 'Bladesover system'. which is now subject to spreading hypertrophy and decay. Scientific invention and commercial enterprise flourish as best they can in the interstices of this structure. George's voyage down the Thames in an experimental torpedo boat at the end of the novel is a symbolic rejection of an England weighed down by its history.

George Ponderevo is not a limited hero like Kipps and Polly, but a first-person narrator whose confused strivings after the ideal of disciplined imagination reflect Wells's own. He finally professes his faith in science, 'the remotest of mistresses' (III, 3, i), but in another respect he is a shameless adventurer, just as his creator was. In a 1911 article, Wells described the literary life as 'one of the modern forms of adventure. Success with a book . . . means in the English-speaking world not merely a moderate financial independence but the utmost freedom of movement and intercourse. One is lifted out of one's narrow circumstances into familiar and unrestrained inter-course with a great variety of people. One sees the world'.[12] After *Tono-Bungay*, the protagonists of his realistic novels also tend to become promiscuous globetrotters. In part, this is an expression of the needs of disciplined imagination: the imperial prospect unfolded by the allegory of Education in *Mr Polly* must be tested and known at first hand by a representative English hero aspiring to full conscious-ness. But it also reflects the change in Wells's experience that accompanied his growing prosperity, and the principle of opportun-ism inherent in autobiographical fiction. Five years after *Tono-Bungay* with its concern with the Condition of England,[13] Wells collected his essays on a variety of topics and gave them the appropriate title *An Englishman Looks at the World*.

III

Certainly he never wrote a conventional travel book. The things that he saw in foreign countries were, on the whole, like the boat riding at anchor off Sandgate beach; they fed his appetite for generalities but had little appeal to the irresponsible side of his imagination. Where he was most effective was in pioneering a certain kind of twentieth-century reportage, in which travel takes the shape of a frustrated but ever-hopeful pilgrimage towards an imagined politi-cal new world. Both *The Future in America* and *Russia in the Shadows* are books of this sort, as are the much less durable *Washington and the Hope of Peace, The New America: The New World*, and his record of a visit to Australasia, *Travels of a Republican Radical in Search of Hot Water*. All these books recount the official travels of one who was already a public figure. It is useless to speculate on what sort of book *The Future in America* might have been had he felt able to confess (as he did in his posthumous volume of autobiography) that, after

12 H. G. Wells, 'Mr Wells Explains Himself', *T.P.'s Magazine* (December 1911). This was written to introduce a Russian edition of his novels. Author's TS., Wells Collection, University of Illinois.

13 See David Lodge, '*Tono-Bungay* and the Condition of England', in *Language of Fiction* (London: Routledge & Kegan Paul, 1966), pp. 214–42.

calling on Theodore Roosevelt at the White House, he had spent the rest of the afternoon with a prostitute. Similarly, his writings about the Soviet Union were never complicated by any analysis of his close relationship with Moura Budberg, who is alleged to have been a Soviet informer.[14]

One clear advantage of *The Future in America* and *Russia in the Shadows* over the novels that were contemporary with them is their sense of history in the making. Nothing that Wells could put into a novel could replace his account of a meeting with Lenin, 'The Dreamer in the Kremlin', even though *The World Set Free* had already included a portrait of a fictional world leader. Nevertheless, the fictional pilgrimage or Grand Tour is an integral part of the sequence of works, beginning with *Ann Veronica* and *The New Machiavelli*, which are usually known as the 'discussion novels' (or 'prig novels') but which increasingly became travelling novels as well. In *Ann Veronica* the heroine's love-affair is sealed by a wordy honeymoon in the Swiss Alps. *The New Machiavelli* returns to the Alps for a high-minded walking-tour. *Marriage* also features an Alpine walking-tour, which proves inconclusive since the hero and heroine, Trafford and Marjorie, abandon their knapsacks in order to enjoy the hospitality of a rich industrialist with a Swiss holiday villa. The Traffords finally decide to make a further pilgrimage to a real wilderness, spending a winter in a hut in the midst of Labrador. Like the Samurai in *A Modern Utopia*, the Traffords need to survive the test of the wilderness in order to emerge as 'new selves' capable of fulfilling their true human potential. International tourism takes the place of the call of the wild in *The Passionate Friends* and *The Research Magnificent*, turgid books which might be described as the ultimate globetrotting novels. Stratton in *The Passionate Friends* goes out to volunteer in the South African War. 'It isn't my business to write here any consecutive story of my war experiences', he tells the reader (5, iii), and it is his general reflections on imperialism and world development which take over the narrative. Later, in similarly reflective vein, he travels to the United States and India (where he survives the obligatory encounter with a tiger), and becomes a frequent visitor to world peace conferences. Much the same is true of Benham in *The Research Magnificent*. After the usual forays to Switzerland and Italy, he decides to go round the world, and sets out for Moscow. Russia to him is merely Britain writ large:

14 See Anthony West, *H. G. Wells: Aspects of a Life*, pp. 143–46.

St Petersburg upon its Neva was like a savage untamed London on a larger Thames; they were sea-gull-haunted tidal cities, like no other capitals in Europe. . . . Like London it looked over the heads of its own people to a limitless polyglot empire. . . . One could draw a score of such contrasted parallels. And now [Russia] was in a state of intolerable stress, that laid bare the elemental facts of a great social organisation. It was having its South African war, its war at the other end of the earth, with a certain defeat instead of a dubious victory . . . . (5, xii)

Once in Moscow, Benham is involved in 'trying to piece together a process, if it was one and the same process, which involved riots in Lodz, fighting at Libau, wild disorder at Odessa, remote colossal battlings in Manchuria, the obscure movements of a disastrous fleet lost somewhere now in the Indian seas' (5, xiii). Meanwhile, his companion is pursuing his relationship with a half-Russian, half-English woman picked up at the Cosmopolis Bazaar. Later, in an increasingly fragmentary narrative, Benham's curiosity takes him to India and China, and then to South Africa, where he is killed in a riot.

In these unsatisfactory works Wells was pioneering an idea of 'revolutionary sightseeing'—a kind of compulsive travelling to the world's trouble-spots—which was later to become a regular feature of twentieth-century life and a source of livelihood for writers and journalists. In *Mr Britling Sees It Through*, however, the Great War virtually confines the Wellsian hero to his country home in Essex, and the novel is all the better for it. For Wells himself, the best that can be said about his sequence of voraciously philosophical globe-trotting protagonists is that they turned his mind to the writing of history. *The Outline of History* was a textbook for the world, intended to supplant the popular nationalistic versions of history which, he believed, had contributed to the catastrophe of the First World War. The *Outline* and its successor *A Short History of the World* have been frequently revised, and continue to be valued—by Asian and American readers, among others—for their attempts to displace Eurocentric versions of world history. Wells's study of history was part and parcel of his search for a new world, since the *Outline* ends not in the present but in the near future. In its original serial publication, the final volume had on its cover a map of the world without political subdivisions, entitled 'The United States of the

World'. The text of the first edition concluded with a discussion of 'The Next Stage in History', arguing for the necessity of a federal world government (pp. 601–08).

IV

If historiography eventually becomes prophecy in Wells's hands, travelogue turns much more quickly into utopian vision. In *A Modern Utopia*, once again, he starts out by using the device of the Swiss walking-tour. As the narrator and his disputatious companion descend the pass leading from Switzerland into Italy, they find that they have been miraculously transported into Utopia, which is represented as a parallel planet at the other end of the galaxy. In due course their explorations bring them back to Utopian London, and, standing in the dignified colonnade which in Utopia corresponds to Trafalgar Square, the new world dissolves and they find themselves back in the familiar city. This is not quite the end of the story, for Wells's narrator, riding away on the top of a bus, imagines the figure of an apocalyptic angel towering over the Haymarket. The trumpet sounds, and he has a momentary vision of 'a world's awakening' to the utopian spirit (p. 369). This vision from the Book of Revelation helps to explain why Wells's literal travel-writing is so much feebler than his accounts of journeys in time or to parallel worlds. What interested him was the promise of a new world, which only the imagination could envisage.

Though *The Future in America* describes a visit to an actual New World and contains some memorable impressions of the United States, it begins and ends with those open-ended invocations of the future—the speculative metaphors, the sense of continuing inquiry, the sentences tailing off into suspension-points—which by 1906 were becoming Wells's trademark. The first chapter poses the aim of his transatlantic voyage as being 'to find whatever consciousness or vague consciousness of a common purpose there may be, what is their Vision, their American Utopia, how much will there is shaping to attain it' (p. 21). At the end of the book, after an exhilarating but inconclusive search for that consciousness of purpose, he describes another apocalyptic fantasy, though this time it is subdued and understated. Looking back at the skyscrapers which already composed the New York skyline, he is irresistibly reminded of 'piled-up packing cases outside a warehouse'. Out of them presently will come 'palaces and noble places', and 'light and fine living', or so he affirms (pp. 358–59). Though this rhetoric is commonplace, the packing-case metaphor momentarily shows Wellsian impatience at its best. He deconstructs New York's monumental buildings and treats them as mere disposable containers for the energies of the people who live in them. Although the New World inevitably failed to measure up to his standards, it remained a source of possible utopian new worlds.

The ultimate new world was the conquest of space. However, space travel tends to appear only as a source of rhetorical uplift at the end of his works. *The First Men in the Moon* was Wells's one contribution to the popular fiction of space adventure. Here the lunar landscapes are dominated by the shock of the sunrise after the long lunar night, and by the hectic growth of vegetation in the low lunar gravity.[15] This is, quite explicitly, a description of a strange new world, compared by the narrator to the miracle of the Creation. The two lunar travellers—the prospector and the disinterested explorer—are engaged on a conventional imperial mission. At times the obstacles they face are comparable to those of a desert or tropical jungle, but the forms and colours of the lunar vegetation are also reminiscent of an enormously distended suburban rock-garden. It is, moreover, a pastoral world, with Selenite shepherds tending the flocks of grazing mooncalves. All this would suggest that Bedford and Cavor have journeyed from Kent, the 'Garden of England', to a place which, however strange, is another garden-world. More familiar garden-worlds are found in some of Wells's visions of the future, from *The Time Machine* to his later utopian books. In 1924 he confessed that his imagination took 'refuge from the slums of to-day in a world like a great garden, various, orderly, lovingly cared-for'.[16] This is plainly an Edenic vision, but it is also a very English one, belonging to the world of (for example) Morris's *News from Nowhere* and Ebenezer Howard's *Garden Cities of To-Morrow*.

In *The Time Machine*, and again in *Men Like Gods*, the urban and industrial landscape has reverted to that of a country park, such as Uppark where Wells's mother was housekeeper and his father had worked as a gardener. The landscape of *The Time Machine* can be appreciated by any visitor to Richmond Park in south-west London. *Men Like Gods* presents another parkland scene, complete with

15 These landscape descriptions were to be lavishly praised by T. S. Eliot. See his article 'Wells as Journalist' (1940), in Patrick Parrinder, ed., *H. G. Wells: The Critical Heritage*, p. 320.

16 H. G. Wells, *A Year of Prophesying* (New York: Macmillan, 1925), p. 351.

distant snow-capped mountains and tame wild cats. A party of earthlings accidentally enters this paradise as a result of a utopian experiment in rotating time-space planes; and they do so from a location in the Home Counties, as they are motoring away from London on the Great West Road. Here, and elsewhere, Wells's anxiety to put southern England behind him is only equalled by his determination that the garden-world which replaces it will be a utopian substitute for the England his characters have left. At such times he reminds us of William Blake, another visionary who sang of building Jerusalem, the perfect city, in the English countryside. Like Wells, Blake in 'The Crystal Cabinet' shows us another England:

> Another England there I saw
> Another London with its Tower
> Another Thames and Other Hills
> And another pleasant Surrey Bower

However, there is another analogy which fits Wells's vision of new worlds, and that is with the pioneer's or colonist's mentality. If the colonist's first priority is to break his or her ties with the homeland, the second priority is to construct a new settlement which at once fulfils the promise of a better society and acts as a memorial to the land that has been left. Some such logic must have inspired the New England settlers, and all the other pioneers in the white-settler lands who gave their new homes in the wilderness familiar British and European names. Wells's deliberate cosmopolitanism and his proclamation of world citizenship remain important and worthwhile ideals, but his deeper affinity is with the New World spirit, even though he himself was never tempted to emigrate. The destruction which many emigrants must have wished on the homelands they were leaving is enacted in *The Time Machine*, *The Invisible Man*, and *The War of the Worlds*, as well as in *Mr Polly*, where the hero's attempted suicide fortuitously succeeds in burning down Fishbourne High Street. In *Tono-Bungay* George Ponderevo is a spiritual emigrant who passes the whole of English society in review before bidding it an embittered farewell. But Wells's novels also anticipate the dreamed-of return to and utopian reconstruction of the homeland—a reconstruction to be achieved by confiscating the land, so to speak, from its present inhabitants, unregenerate members of the human species who have failed to evolve into World-Men. So his utopianism continues to be marked by its origins in an age of imperialism. But it is this prophetic sense of otherness superimposed on Englishness, of an old world irresistibly giving way to an imagined new one, which inspires some of Wells's best writing.

CHAPTER SEVEN
Utopia and Meta-Utopia

I

In *Experiment in Autobiography* Wells includes an apologetic discussion of his dealings with the novel, based on material first asssembled together in a folder labelled ' "Whether I am a Novelist" ' (II, p. 487). I should like to believe that somewhere among his unsorted papers there is a comparable folder, labelled 'Whether I am a Utopian'. For though in his lifetime the 'Wellsian Utopia' was almost as famous as Freudian psychology or Platonic love, in retrospect his relationship to the utopian mode seems uneasy and paradoxical. He was a major propagandist for utopian ideas who never produced a major utopian book. *A Modern Utopia* is the nearest thing in his corpus to that book, but it has so far failed to achieve canonical status either within the utopian genre or among Wells's own best-known writings. His uneasiness with the utopian mode is hardly surprising in one who started out as an author of dystopias or ironic utopias, beginning with *The Time Machine* which seems intended to superannuate previous utopian texts. A comparable unease can be found near the end of his life, in his 1939 radio broadcast on 'Utopias' given in Australia, and not printed in full until forty years later. Here he sharply contrasts the utopia with the 'anticipatory tale'. Utopias are dreams—'The Utopian story imagines a better and a happier world and makes no pretence to reality'—whereas anticipatory tales 'profess to foretell—more often than not, with warnings and forebodings'. The utopia, he suggests, has an imaginative permanence denied to the sort of novel he himself writes:

> 'If only'—that is the Utopian key-note. There is little prospect of any futuristic writings becoming permanent literature. We prophets write for our own time and pass almost before we are dead, but some of the Utopias are among the most enduring gems in the literary treasure house. They throw down no such self-destructive challenge as the futurist writer does, when he says, 'This is the way

things are going—and this is what is coming about'. The Utopian says merely, 'If only', and escapes from time, death and judgment. (p. 117)

Here Wells (with a characteristic note of artistic self-deprecation) names himself as a prophet, not as a utopian. The utopian writer produces speculative fictions about the good society which escape from 'time, death and judgment'. We can see from this why the utopian mood, in Wells, is always precarious and vulnerable. The finest of his own speculative fictions were not dreams of utopia but explorations of time, with a message of *memento mori*.

At the end of his talk on 'Utopias' he moves from considering individual utopian visions to the collective utopianism of scientists. Plato and More are replaced by Roger and Francis Bacon and their disciples. The problem here is that the idea of a scientific utopia is a paradox, if not an actual contradiction in terms. Science is an inherently dynamic force, relying (as Wells puts it) on 'the perpetual criticism, increase and diffusion of more knowledge and more' (p. 120). The effect must be to subvert any stable social order. Wells's rejection of a static utopianism is one of the premises of *A Modern Utopia*, and he repeated it throughout his life: in the words of Chapter 7 of *The Open Conspiracy*, 'No Stable Utopia is Contemplated'.[1] Social instability and the individual disturbance that it causes are two of the principal evils that earlier utopians, up to and including William Morris, had set out to remove. One of the reasons why we cannot mistake *A Modern Utopia* for a classic utopian text safe from time, death and judgment is that the society it outlines is not the crystallisation of a personal vision but a dynamic and synthetic construction. The political doctrines of Wells's book are lucidly set out, but can lay few claims to originality. Today they present a somewhat dated appearance (not least because they were superseded by some of his own later work) and it is for its textual and imaginative qualities, rather than its political ideas, that *A Modern Utopia* most repays study.

II

My use of the term 'meta' in this chapter is indebted to Hayden White's study of nineteenth-century historicism, *Metahistory*. White

1 H. G. Wells, *The Open Conspiracy: Blue Prints for a World Revolution* (London: Gollancz, 1928), pp. 51–52.

foregoes the common use of 'meta' to denote a manifest self-consciousness in discourse—the sense in which metalanguage is language discussing language, and metafiction is fiction that draws attention to its own fictionality. Instead he is concerned to unravel the latent or hidden elements of discursive structure. Thus he is not primarily interested in a historian's explicit use of theoretical concepts and criticism of previous historians, but in what he calls the latent metahistorical elements—'a deep structural content which is generally poetic, and specifically linguistic, in nature, and which serves as the precritically accepted paradigm of what a distinctively "historical" explanation should be'.[2] In the case of Wells, both the manifest and latent senses of meta-utopia need to be borne in mind.[3] A reading of the manifestly self-reflexive strategy of *A Modern Utopia* will lead to a consideration of the poetics of Wells's utopianism as a whole.

The Utopia of *A Modern Utopia* is a distant planet in a far solar system, which just happens to be physically identical to the earth, and which is inhabited at this unique moment in time by a population genetically identical to that of earth. This means that everyone on earth possesses a 'double' in Utopia. Wells's use of the form of the travelogue resembles some of his other utopian and dystopian novels, but in fact *A Modern Utopia* is not usually counted among his fictional works. Utopian writing is always a mixed form—a hybrid between disciplined exposition and irresponsible imaginative freedom—but Wells carried generic disjunction to extraordinary lengths, writing that he aimed at 'a sort of shot-silk texture between philosophical discussion on the one hand and imaginative narrative on the other' (p. viii). The narrative element (the wanderings of the narrator and his companion) is deliberately presented as a kind of game, an imagined visit to a fictive place constructed according to rules and assumptions which are clearly set out and defended.[4] In a

2 Hayden White, *Metahistory: The Historical Imagination in Nineteenth-Century Europe* (Baltimore: Johns Hopkins University Press, 1973), p. ix.

3 This should not be confused, however, with the use of the term 'meta-utopia' by some political scientists who seem quite innocent of the idea that a utopia is a particular kind of text rather than a kind of society. See for example Robert Nozick, *Anarchy, State and Utopia* (Oxford: Oxford University Press, 1974), pp. 297ff.

4 Indeed, David Y. Hughes has argued that 'Wells's notion of a utopia more nearly approaches to a hypothesis awaiting testing than to a "place" '. 'The Mood of *A Modern Utopia*', *Extrapolation* 19 (December 1977), p. 60.

frame narrative, Wells suggests that we might visualise the whole text as an illustrated lecture, given by someone called 'The Owner of the Voice', whose subject is the 'adventure of his soul among Utopian inquiries' (p. 2). And in his 1939 radio broadcast Wells described *A Modern Utopia* as a 'summary of Utopian ideas' (p. 120).

The motif of summarising utopian ideas appears elsewhere in Wells's work. We may connect the 'Owner of the Voice' in *A Modern Utopia* with a strangely charismatic scholar and sage, Mr Sempack, who figures in *Meanwhile*, a novel dealing with such topics of its day as the rise of Italian Fascism and the British General Strike. Mr Sempack has been 'reading and writing about all the Utopias in the world', and he is what Wells calls a 'Utopographer' (I, 1). For Wells, the utopographer was one of the unacknowledged legislators of the world. In a 1906 essay he had attacked the positivist social science of Spencer and Comte, arguing that comparative utopography (on the model of comparative anatomy) would be the central discipline of sociology. 'I figure to myself . . . a sort of dream book of huge dimensions, in reality perhaps dispersed in many volumes by many hands, upon the Ideal Society. This book, this picture of the perfect state, would be the backbone of sociology'.[5]

Utopography, in these terms, is not an individual but a collective project. Nevertheless, *A Modern Utopia* is a highly personal sketch for Wells's dream-book. In between the spurts of fictional travelogue it offers a sustained comparative discussion making systematic reference to about twenty previous utopian writers, as well as to utopian sects, utopian architects, utopian communities, and utopian languages. Plato is the writer most often referred to, followed by More, Morris, Comte, Bacon, Cabet, Campanella, and Bellamy. Curiously, the branch of utopian thought least well represented in *A Modern Utopia* is that of the early utopian socialists, Fourier, Owen, and Saint-Simon. But Wells made good this omission three years later in Chapter 10 of his popular exposition of socialism, *New Worlds for Old*.

III

Why did Wells base his utopia on such an explicit scheme of meta-utopian references? In *A Modern Utopia* he was less concerned with predicting the future than with joining in the age-old argument about the nature of the good society. (In the same spirit, he would

5 H. G. Wells, 'The So-Called Science of Sociology', in *An Englishman Looks at the World* (London: Cassell, 1914), p. 205.

later distinguish between utopias and 'futuristic writings'.) He had already moved from fictional prophecy to what would now be called futurological writing in a series of books published immediately before *A Modern Utopia*: *Anticipations, Mankind in the Making* and *The Discovery of the Future*. These were the books that made his reputation as a political thinker. *A Modern Utopia*, however, is set not in the future but in an alternative present. This is in sharp contrast not only to Wells's 'anticipations' but to the futuristic works of Bellamy and Morris, his immediate predecessors in utopian socialism. A provisional assessment might be that in *A Modern Utopia* Wells for once was forswearing prophecy.

In its place, the book exhibits what would become the familiar Wellsian technique of synthetic remodelling or synthetic modernisation—the self-conscious revision and updating of an earlier text or textual tradition. That he was not alone in the impulse to modernise can be seen from such influential contemporary works as W. H. Mallock's *The New Republic* (1877) and G. Lowes Dickinson's *A Modern Symposium* (1905), not to mention Havelock Ellis's *The New Spirit* (1890) and A. R. Orage's journal *The New Age*. But Wells's manifest commitment to synthetic modernisation outdid any of his literary rivals. Before writing *A Modern Utopia* he had already named the world state that he championed in *Anticipations* and *Mankind in the Making* the 'New Republic'. His later 'remodelled' books include *The New Machiavelli, The Undying Fire* based on the Book of Job, and *The Anatomy of Frustration: A Modern Synthesis*, based on Burton's *Anatomy of Melancholy*. A more extended list would add *When the Sleeper Wakes* as a sardonic riposte to Bellamy's *Looking Backward, The Great State* by Wells and other ex-Fabians as an attempt to rewrite *Fabian Essays, Boon* as a parody of Mallock's *The New Republic, The Rights of Man* as a modernisation of Tom Paine, and the assortment of late works in which he borrowed his structural idea from Voltaire's *Candide* (*Mr Blettsworthy on Rampole Island* and *All Aboard for Ararat*) or from Morris's *A Dream of John Ball* (*'42 to '44* and *The Happy Turning*). Put together, these works seem to locate Wells in an eclectic tradition of learned, radical 'gadflies on the state' ranging from Plato and More to Bellamy and Morris: a tradition that is perhaps foreshadowed by his student article on Socrates[6] and which vividly illustrates his refusal to be confined within any single artistic

6 Herbert G. Wells, 'Socrates', *Science Schools Journal* I:1 (December 1886), pp. 18–21.

genre. These books are, in fact, a remarkable demonstration of his literary heterodoxy.

Wells expounds his belief in the underlying principle of synthesis in 'Scepticism of the Instrument', the appendix to *A Modern Utopia* which offers a personal statement of the metaphysical creed that he had arrived at via the study of biology and geology. Huxley's teaching had led him to posit the uniqueness and transience of all organic and inorganic matter; from this it followed that all systems of logic and classification were inherently provisional. Such a creed, as he recognised, brought him close to the contemporary Pragmatist school and especially to the philosophy of William James. At intervals throughout his life he restated his 'Neo-Nominalism', which he claimed as a necessary starting-point for experimental science.[7] He does not offer his Pragmatism and Nominalism as fixed positions but as working assumptions, instruments for the construction of a world-picture. A crude way of representing this universal picture would be to imagine a vast jumble of jigsaw-puzzle pieces, each different from its neighbour, but each slowly and imperceptibly changing its shape so that the pattern of the whole is not constant. Yet at any given moment there is a discoverable pattern, and the task of the human species is to fit the pieces together and to resist the temptation to kick the whole puzzle to smithereens. The pattern of the finished jigsaw is a utopia. With all the pieces scattered round him on the floor, childish, half-grown *homo sapiens* struggles to emerge from what Wells frequently calls the 'Age of Confusion'. At best present-day utopography is, like Mr Sempack's conversation in *Meanwhile*, 'a fitting together of the main creative suggestions for the regulation of human affairs that have accumulated' (I, 4). Will this be enough to solve the jigsaw puzzle? The doubt is expressed by another character in the same novel:

> 'This ultimate reasonableness of Sempack's is a rare thing, a hothouse plant. It's the last fine distillation of human hope. It lives in just a few happy corners of the world, in libraries and liberal households. If you smash the greenhouse glass or turn off the hot water it will die. How is it ever coming into the open air . . . ?' (II, 10)

7 See for example H. G. Wells, *First and Last Things* (London: Constable, 1908); *The Work, Wealth and Happiness of Mankind* (London: Heinemann, 1932), pp. 63–69; *The Conquest of Time*, pp. 34–40.

The first move in the process of synthetic remodelling in *A Modern Utopia* is to brush aside what Wells saw as the purely hedonistic utopianism of Morris's *News from Nowhere*. Morris had felt free to change 'the nature of man and the nature of things together' (p. 7), whereas the fictive world of *A Modern Utopia* is one in which human 'culture' has been transformed without in the least altering human 'nature'. This may appear a controversial and self-defeating exercise, but it is only an exercise, and Wells openly concedes its artificiality. His aim is to produce a society different from Morris's, in which human aggression and competitiveness are controlled and contained within an elaborate framework of social order. As a modern liberal, he sets out to show that social order can be upheld in a utopia guaranteeing individual liberty, freedom of movement, freedom of expression, privacy, freedom from drudgery, and control of personal property—though not universal suffrage. The framework of centralised controls includes a money economy, an advanced technology, a humane penal system, regulated marriage, population planning, sanitation, health-care, state supported child-care, central data storage, institutionalised wage-bargaining, and a post-Christian synthetic religion. All these points show a marked modernity of outlook, with the single exception of the refusal of universal elective democracy. The vote is restricted, we discover, to a body of people whose presence at the centre of *A Modern Utopia* is a bold and striking anomaly. For the nucleus of this modernised collectivist state is an institution as archaic and hierarchical as it is possible to conceive—a clerisy or secular priesthood modelled on Plato's Guardians, who 'look like Knights Templars, who bear a name that recalls the swordsmen of Japan' (p. 277)—the *samurai*. The main narrative drive of *A Modern Utopia* comes not so much from its exposition of the ideas of the welfare state (far-sighted though this may have been), but from the narrator's desire not to leave this new world without meeting his utopian double. Necessarily, his double turns out to be one of the *samurai*. Their meeting embodies both the allure and the impossibility of the Wellsian 'synthesis'.

The double is at once identical with the narrator, and utterly different from him. The reader was presented with a comparable identity-paradox at the beginning of the book, since the narrator himself, a plump blue-eyed sparrow of a man whose voice is an 'unattractive tenor that becomes at times aggressive' (p. 2), is an easily recognisable caricature of H. G. Wells: he is both Wells and not-Wells. He is called 'The Owner of the Voice', and this curious locution doubtless implies that the Voice may, at some point, break free of its owner. For the first two-thirds of the book there is no sign of this happening. Then in Chapters 8 and 9, as the meeting with the double approaches, we encounter some curious hesitations. Chapter 8, 'My Utopian Self', mainly consists of conversations between the narrator and his travelling-companion, a botanist; Chapter 9 shows the narrator referring to Wells himself, as a 'literary man' who had foreseen a revolutionary organisation on *samurai* lines in the 'New Republic' of *Anticipations* and *Mankind in the Making* (p. 263). But as this chapter—the literary core of *A Modern Utopia*—proceeds, the expository voice passes from the narrator to his Utopian counterpart, who tells of the nature and outlook of the *samurai*. At this point we are no longer reading an explicit meta-utopia, a summary of 'personal adventures among Utopian philosophies', since the speaking voice in the text offers not suggestion and speculation but intimate knowledge. This is not utopography but Utopianism—or should we say the return of prophecy? The voice of the *samurai*, however, is very quickly cut off. The next chapter is a fine but straighforward piece of Wellsian journalism on the topic of 'Race in Utopia', and then 'The Bubble Bursts' (p. 352) and the narrator and the botanist find themselves back on earth.

IV

Throughout the book the narrative drive offered by the writer's search for his utopian double has been countered by the resistance set up by the botanist, who expresses humanity's recalcitrance in the face of the utopian spirit. 'The old Utopists never had to encumber themselves with this sort of man' (p. 179), the narrator complains; but 'there's no getting away from him in this life' (p. 343). The dream-journey comes to its abrupt end when the botanist finds the double he is looking for—that of his former lover—and she is, needless to say, accompanied by another man. It is his intense emotional disturbance which leads to the bursting of the bubble. The return to earth takes place at the very moment when the narrator is most confident in his possession of utopia and in his expectation of more and more certain knowledge:

> As I walk along the river terrace to the hotel where the botanist awaits me, and observe the Utopians I encounter, I have no thought that my tenure of Utopia becomes every moment more precarious. There float in my mind vague

anticipations of more talks with my double and still more, of a steady elaboration of detail, of interesting journeys of exploration. I forget that a Utopia is a thing of the imagination that becomes more fragile with every added circumstance, that like a soap-bubble, it is most brilliantly and variously coloured at the very instant of its dissolution. (p. 352)

A soap-bubble bursts when the synthetic equilibrium of forces determining its shape and suspension suddenly breaks down. These forces, I suggest, are the latent meta-utopian elements determining the Wellsian utopia.

The first meta-utopian element is, curiously enough, one that Wells ostentatiously dismisses at the beginning of *A Modern Utopia*— the vision of the earthly paradise, whose modern advocate was William Morris. This was always more attractive to Wells than he really cared to admit. The manner of Morris's dismissal is in itself a confession of this: 'Were we free to have our untrammelled desire, . . . we should make the whole race wise, tolerant, noble, perfect— wave our hands to a splendid anarchy, every man doing as it pleases him, and none pleased to do evil, in a world as good in its essential nature, as ripe and sunny, as the world before the Fall' (p. 7). Visions in which the whole human race or its descendants—not just, as in *A Modern Utopia*, part of it—have been made, or appear to have been made, 'wise, tolerant, noble, perfect' appear at least twice in Wells's fiction. There is not only the fleeting vision of the world of the Eloi as a communistic Arcadia at the beginning of *The Time Machine*, but the portrayal of a more genuinely arcadian paradise in his later utopian romance *Men Like Gods*. Here Wells shows the species at a higher level of evolution, living under a form of anarchism. The utopians' intellectual capacity is reflected in unimaginable (and, on Wells's part, unimagined) achievements in science and in the arts. They communicate by means of telepathic mindspeech. These utopians are the natural descendants of the intellectual aristocracy, the 'fine Olympians'[8] whom Wells saw as the highest products of the civilisation of the English country-house. Their utopia is almost destroyed by the belligerence of a party of English visitors, led by a

8 H. G. Wells, *Tono-Bungay*, I, 1, iii. Cf. *Experiment in Autobiography*, I, p. 136, where the country-house is described as 'the expermental cellule of the coming Modern State'.

splendid caricature of Winston Churchill—the unacceptable face of the country-house ethic.

Mr Barnstaple, Wells's protagonist, says of the utopia of *Men Like Gods* that ' "By all outward appearance this might be a Communism such as was figured in a book we used to value on Earth, a book called *News from Nowhere* by an Earthling named William Morris. It was a graceful impossible book" ' (III, 2, iv). Something that Wells can hardly have failed to notice in *News from Nowhere* is its idyllic portrayal of sexual relationships. A defining feature of the earthly paradise in Wells is that, going further than Morris, he shows his utopians enjoying complete freedom from the emotional disturbances caused by sexual passion. In *The Time Machine* there is the brother-and-sister relationship between the Time Traveller and Weena. The hero of *The History of Mr Polly*, having survived a suicide bid, a major fire, and three desperate fights, finds peace and contentment at the Potwell Inn, a mildly Rabelaisian paradise which he inhabits on terms of asexual companionship with a character known only as the Fat Woman. Wells's two formal utopias, *A Modern Utopia* and *Men Like Gods*, were each followed a year later by a sort of unofficial pendant, *In the Days of the Comet* and *The Dream* respectively—novels stressing not the perfection of social organisation in a utopia, but the contrast between the individual contentment it would offer and the emotional storm and stress of twentieth-century life. (In addition, the two 'pendant' novels unlike the formal utopias are plotted on a time-axis between present and future.) *The Dream* describes a vision of present-day life experienced by Sarnac, an Olympian living in AD 4000 who is staying with his mistress Sunray and their friends at a holiday resort. In his dream, Sarnac becomes Harry Mortimer Smith, an embattled twentieth-century citizen whose emotional turmoil ends in his becoming the victim of a crime of passion. The dream is scarcely comprehensible to the Olympians, whose life consists in rational, non-possessive sexual companionship in a state of continual nudity. Just as this follows out the implications of *Men Like Gods* for individual life, so *In the Days of the Comet* builds on the botanist's experience in *A Modern Utopia*, showing how the coming of the earthly paradise supersedes sexual possessiveness and the problem of jealousy. *In the Days of the Comet* is narrated by Willie Leadford, a young man from the Potteries who becomes murderously jealous after his girl-friend, Nettie, goes off with another man. After the 'Change' brought about by the green vapours of the comet, Willie is at first as unreceptive to utopian ideas of sexuality as the botanist had been. When Nettie proposes to divide her attentions between her old lover and her new one, Willie is unable to accept, and goes back home to his mother. Finally, however, his infatuation is cured and he becomes a contented participant in a foursome with Nettie, his male rival, and a new partner, Anna Reeves, who becomes the mother of his children. For Willie the rites of passage to utopian sexuality include the renewal of his relationship with his mother, her death, and the transference of his affections to Anna who has been his mother's nurse. It is a regression to childlike love: 'I turned to Anna as a child may turn to its nurse', he recalls. 'She whispered to me, "There, there!" as one whispers comfort to a child. . . .' (III, 3, iii). There is, perhaps, a similarly regressive and childlike element in all Wells's representations of utopian sexuality. The Fat Woman in *Mr Polly* is a mother-substitute, and Weena like all the Eloi is there to be treated as a pet or baby sister. Sexually, at least, Wells is at one with William Morris in representing the earthly paradise as a place of 'second childhood', an 'epoch of rest' where humanity is stuck, becalmed if not actually degenerating.[9]

In the new society of *In the Days of the Comet* it is not the male characters but the women, Nettie and Anna, who take the sexual initiative. This contrasts with the institutional relationship between the sexes in *A Modern Utopia*, since Wells's formal utopia is, all too evidently, an idealised patriarchy. The Utopian marriage laws insist on the chastity of the wife. Women are allowed to join the *samurai*, but there is also a 'Lesser Rule' open to women—that is, *samurai* wives—alone. Gender difference is enshrined in the religion and mythology of the new order. The Utopians worship both the state (male) and Nature, 'the stark mother', to whom 'civilised men' (the *samurai*) go back on an annual pilgrimage (p. 304). The Utopian coin bears the head of Newton on one side, and, on the reverse, the allegory of Peace as a beautiful woman. In *Men Like Gods*, however, Wells abandons such patriarchal trappings and constructs what appears to be a genuinely equal society. The earthlings arrive in utopia as the result of a failed scientific experiment in which the two researchers, a man and a woman, have been killed. The names of these 'two beautiful young people' (I, 3, ii) are Arden and Green-

---

9 William Morris, *News from Nowhere*, ed. James Redmond (London: Routledge & Kegan Paul, 1970), p. 87. 'An epoch of rest' is the subtitle of Morris's 'utopian romance'.

lake—names which play down the gender difference and which suggest the possibility that Wells had moved closer to an androgynous ideal.

No sooner has Wells created an earthly paradise than he or his characters feel moved to destroy it. V. S. Pritchett wrote that 'There are always fist-fights and fires in the early Wells. Above all, there are fires'.[10] The fires symbolise the potentially unharnessable energy released by the technological exploitation of nature. Mankind is the 'fire-making animal', as Wells puts it in the chapter of *The World Set Free* which introduces the discovery of nuclear energy and is, significantly, entitled 'The Sun Snarers' (Prelude, i). Fires in Wells are almost always deliberately started. The Time Traveller sets off a conflagration with his stolen lump of camphor. The Martians in *The War of the Worlds* start fires by means of the Heat-Ray. Mr Polly sets his own house on fire. Arden and Greenlake are killed by an explosion. Lurking in these examples is the suggestion that humankind is strengthened by going through the fire (it is a measure of the degeneracy of the Morlocks and of Weena that they perish so miserably by it). *In the Days of the Comet* shows an interesting attempt by Wells to turn the purging fire into a wholly positive symbol. There the new age opens with the semi-annual Beltane festivals in which all the accumulated materials of life before the Change are systematically burnt. The only articles to be spared these 'Phoenix fires' (III, 3, i) are carefully disinfected and preserved in museums.

Very different, however, are the Wellsian fist-fights, which symbolise human recalcitrance and resistance to utopia. The unregenerate belligerence and competitiveness of the human species appears on two principal levels, those of nationalism or imperialism and of sexuality. In *Men Like Gods* Catskill (Churchill) and his party almost destroy utopia as a result of their attempts to colonise it and plant the League of Nations flag. In *A Modern Utopia* and *In the Days of the Comet*, sexual rapacity is the destroying force. While the scientific romances contain many scenes of actual fist-fights, the 'soap-bubble' of *A Modern Utopia* is pricked by a virtual fist-fight, due to the botanist's jealous rage when he sees his beloved's double and her companion. The narrator has to apply both verbal and physical restraints as the botanist goes white, 'his thin hand is clenched' (p. 355), and he

10 V. S. Pritchett, 'The Scientific Romances', in Bernard Bergonzi, ed., *H. G. Wells: A Collection of Critical Essays* (Englewood Cliffs, N.J.: Prentice-Hall, 1976), p. 32.

'waves an unteachable destructive arm' (p. 357). At the moment when the fight is about to erupt, Utopia vanishes. Wells, it seems, cannot portray a paradisal society without an ironic sub-plot asserting the perpetuity of aggressions as it is realised in the violence and self-assertion of the contemporary world. Often, too, violence and self-assertion in his novels have an evident survival-value. It is only in advanced technological societies that these qualities threaten species destruction.

V

In the poetics of the Wellsian utopia the Morrisian vision of an earthly paradise occurs in the mode of metaphor—beautiful and alluring, but always insubstantial or illusory. The earthly paradise may be a delusion (as in *The Time Machine*), a parallel world based on a simile (as in *Men Like Gods*), or a promised land coming after great and fearful changes (as in *In the Days of the Comet* and, at a different level, *Mr Polly*). The destructive element, based on the intervention of unregenerate mankind, is—with the exception of some of Wells's fire-symbolism—presented in the ironic mode. Bernard Bergonzi has spoken of Wells's early scientific romances as 'ironic myths',[11] and, so far, my account of his meta-utopianism reveals a conventional Wellsian dualism of optimism and pessimism, or metaphor and irony. But there is a third element that is integral to Wells's utopianism, and which has still to be accounted for.[12]

At the beginning of *Songs of Experience*, William Blake—one of the poets studied by Wells at South Kensington when he should have

11 Bernard Bergonzi, '*The Time Machine*: An Ironic Myth', in *H. G. Wells: A Collection of Critical Essays*, pp. 39–55.

12 Many critics have viewed Wells's imagination as a theatre of dualistic conflict; for a persuasive example, see John Huntington, *The Logic of Fantasy: H. G. Wells and Science Fiction* (New York: Columbia University Press, 1982). Hayden White's interpretative system in *Metahistory*, on the other hand, shows a rigid attachment to fourfold categories. My own threefold hypothesis is indebted to Leon Stover, who in 'Spade House Dialectic: Theme and Theory in "Things to Come"', *Wellsian* ns5 (1982), pp. 23–32, draws attention to Wells's interest in the symbolism of the Hindu trinity. In the argument that follows, Vishnu (the preserver) corresponds to the metaphorical element, Siva (the destroyer) to the ironic, and Brahma (the builder) to the synthetic.

been revising for his Finals[13]—evokes the Garden of Eden in the following lines:

> Hear the voice of the Bard!
> Who Present, Past & Future sees;
> Whose ears have heard
> The Holy Word
> That walk'd among the ancient trees . . .

In Wells there is a Garden of Eden—the metaphor of a sexually innocent earthly paradise—and also an ironic destructive force, the serpent of human recalcitrance. But there is also a prophetic voice, the voice of the Bard. After his return from Utopia to London the narrator of *A Modern Utopia* sees the apocalyptic angel, 'a towering figure of flame and colour, standing between earth and sky, with a trumpet in his hands, over there above the Haymarket, against the October glow; and when he sounds, all the *samurai*, all who are *samurai* in Utopia, will know themselves and one another. . . .' (pp. 368–69). Though the image refers to the Book of Revelation, it also seems to allude to the ending of Book 9 of Plato's *Republic*, which states that '[the city] is laid up as a pattern in heaven, which he who desires may behold, and beholding, may set his own house in order. . . . for he will live after the manner of that city, having nothing to do with any other'.[14]

The force of prophecy lies in the voice or writings of the prophet: the angel's trumpet, the soothsayer's cryptic message, the writings on Sibylline leaves. While the content of Wells's future visions varies enormously, they are all presented, to some extent, in an oracular manner. The dream-narrative within a dream-narrative (as in *In the Days of the Comet*) is a frequent device, allowing him to intrude the devices of foretelling into a story that, in terms of his own distinction cited at the beginning of this chapter, is technically utopian rather than futuristic. Even in *A Modern Utopia*, as we have seen, he subverts intellectual utopography at the moment when he gives to his speculations the authority of a Voice disconnected from its Owner. For if the narrator, the 'Owner of the Voice', is an expository device, the voice of his Utopian double is comparatively displaced and oracular.

13 H. G. Wells, *Experiment in Autobiography*, I, p. 241.
14 R. M. Hare and D. A. Russell, eds., *The Dialogues of Plato*, trans. Benjamin Jowett (London: Sphere, 1970), IV, p. 387.

Wells's utopian worlds are joined to our empirical world either in space (the parallel world somewhere else in the cosmos) or, in what I have called the pendant novels, in time. This means that, far from simply negating our empirical world or forming an ironic antithesis to it, they fit together with our world into a greater whole. Utopia is a 'hopeful stage, leading to a long ascent of stages' (*A Modern Utopia*, p. 5); it is 'but one of countless universes that move together in time, that lie against one another, endlessly like the leaves of a book' (*Men Like Gods*, III, 4, vi). To know all these stages, worlds, or universes would necessitate the development of a synthetic human consciousness, infinitely extensible in space and time, capable of reading the whole of creation as if it were the books in a library. The Wellsian motifs of space and time travel are, therefore, not metaphoric or ironic but synthetic or synecdochic. Each world that he invents or that his protagonists visit is a 'part' whose ultimate significance lies in its belonging to a greater whole. No Wellsian utopia is an end in itself, and no paradise is ever conclusively lost or regained. Behind each individual manifestation of the utopian spirit is an ultimate utopia based on 'developments of power and activity upon which at present we can set no limits nor give any certain form'.[15] A number of Wells's texts end with the expression of an open-ended cosmic mysticism which promises knowledge of the super-universe consisting of all the topias and utopias possible to human beings or their descendants.

In *A Modern Utopia* this all-embracing synthetic vision finds expression in the voice of the narrator's double, who speaks on behalf of the *samurai*. Describing his annual journey into the wilderness, he falls into the cosmic rhetoric which Wells had earlier invoked in *The Discovery of the Future*. It is significant that in Utopia the conquest of space is an aspiration of the *samurai* élite, not of humanity as a whole; for, as we saw earlier, the position of the *samurai* is anomalous. Their movement was conceived as a revolutionary movement, which made Utopia into a world state. For all their hierarchical privileges, are they still in effect a revolutionary group? Whatever they are, they cannot simply be (like Plato's Guardians) the efficient rulers of a stable society. Through the device of the double Wells strongly suggests that they continue to display a radical energy, and that their projects, if realised, would transform if not destroy the painstakingly constructed society which is subject to

15 H. G. Wells, *The Open Conspiracy*, p. 51.

their rule. The *samurai* are revolutionaries and foretellers installed, somewhat uncomfortably, at the heart of Utopia.

VI

At the end of Wells's book the angel of the resurrection summons the *samurai* from 'above the Haymarket'. Significantly, Wells was unable to keep his conception of a voluntary élite within the pages of *A Modern Utopia*. People wrote to him, offering themselves as *samurai*. Younger members of the Fabian Society especially liked to cast themselves in this role.[16] Later, in the 1920s and 1930s, Wells revived the idea, under the name of the Open Conspiracy. (This was to be a revolutionary pressure-group of liberal democrats modelled in part on the disciplined élites of the Soviet Communist Party and the Italian Fascists.) Some earlier utopians, especially the socialists Cabet and Bellamy, had been still more successful than Wells in stirring up public controversy and winning support. But whereas in their case it was the portrayal of a whole society that captured the readers' imagination, in Wells's it was perhaps not so much Utopia as the vision of the disciplined élite. (A chapter in his *Experiment in Autobiography* is revealingly titled 'The Samurai—in Utopia and in the Fabian Society'). The *samurai* are detachable from the Modern Utopia, and their awareness of the human predicament goes far beyond the temporary structure of social institutions and policies over which they preside.

In his 1939 essay on utopias, Wells was to argue that scientific workers were the true modern utopians. In *A Modern Utopia* the *samurai* share the pessimistic view of humanity's place in the cosmos which was, for Wells in 1905, still an inevitable outcome of scientific thinking. They are preoccupied with the Second Law of Thermodynamics with its prospect of a ' "time when our sun will be red and dull, and air and water will lie frozen together in a common snowfield where now the forests of the tropics are steaming. . ." ' (p. 307). In *The War of the Worlds* Wells had created another society facing the consequences of the Law of Entropy—the Martians, grotesque parodies of the 'Man of the Year Million', who were forced by the cooling of their planet to search for another home closer to the sun. Like the Martians, and like Wells himself, the *samurai* see space travel, and ultimately star travel, as the only way of escaping

16 For the 'Samurai Societies' see David C. Smith, *H. G. Wells: Desperately Mortal*, p. 101.

ultimate extinction. If this is so, Utopian comfort and stability is delusive, and must give way to restless, dissatisfied imaginings.

The fundamental premise of the classical utopia is that the human being is a political animal, whose highest purposes can be achieved through the perfection of social organisation. For Wells, however, it would be more accurate to say that he or she is a cosmic animal, whose purpose is to maintain and extend its biological empire in the face of hostile forces that it can never wholly subjugate. This cosmic viewpoint, inherited from Huxley and Darwin, is in some ways decisively anti-utopian. However, the dynamism and instability of Wells's Modern Utopia are shared by the earlier 'scientific utopias', such as Bacon's *New Atlantis*, which stress the unlimited pursuit of increased knowledge and power over nature. This must have revolutionary, or at least destabilising, social effects. Wells, by endowing his *samurai* with a prophetic social mission, makes explicit what in Bacon's utopia is merely a submerged implication. (On the face of it the elaborate ceremonial trappings of Solomon's House, Bacon's scientific research institute, make *The New Atlantis* one of the most conservative and hierarchical of all utopias.) With the voice of the *samurai*, *A Modern Utopia* abandons the utopian tradition and heralds, instead, twentieth-century science fiction as a literature of cosmic foreboding. Fortunate accidents—miracle visitors, heroic space exploits, magical discoveries, friendly or easily subjugated aliens—may help to ensure human survival in the short term (which is what matters within the conventions of adventure fiction), but can do little to affect our ultimate fate. Olaf Stapledon, Isaac Asimov, Arthur C. Clarke, Robert Heinlein, J. G. Ballard and Philip K. Dick all produce future-oriented narratives of this sort. A more recent generation of science-fiction writers has, like Wells, attempted to annex the utopian tradition. The test of all such works is the role that they allot to scientific rationality and the search for knowledge. It seems that it would need nothing short of a new epistemology, a new and less dynamic and power-driven construction of the scientific enterprise, to remove the lurking incompatibility between utopia and the literature of scientific futurology.

PART II
Wells's Legacy

CHAPTER EIGHT
The Future as Anti-Utopia:
Wells, Zamyatin and Orwell

I

Michael Glenny has written that 'the essential link in the English "anti-Utopian" tradition—the man who grasped the potential in the literary technique of an English writer of one generation, gave it a new dimension and handed it on to two masters of the next generation—was that curiously "English" Russian, Yevgeny Zamyatin'.[1] The English writer of an earlier generation was Wells, and the two later masters were Aldous Huxley and George Orwell. Orwell himself acknowledged that *Nineteen Eighty-Four* was indebted to Zamyatin's *We* (1920–21), and asserted that Huxley must have drawn upon it in *Brave New World*.[2] (Huxley always denied this.) Another critic, the science-fiction scholar Mark Hillegas, locates Zamyatin in the modern anti-utopian tradition beginning with Wells and extending through Huxley, Orwell, E. M. Forster, C. S. Lewis and the Czech writer Karel Capek. Hillegas shows that the topography of Zamyatin's dehumanised city-state, with its huge apartment blocks, its dictatorship, its walls excluding the natural world and its weird House of Antiquity, is built of elements from *When the Sleeper Wakes*, 'A Story of the Days to Come' and *The Time Machine*.[3] Zamyatin's annexation as, so to speak, an honorary English anti-

1 Michael Glenny, 'Introduction' to Yevgeny Zamyatin, *We*, trans. Bernard Guilbert Guerney (London: Cape, 1970), p. 22. Subsequent page references in the text are to this edition of *We*. However, I have also consulted the translation by Mirra Ginsburg (New York: Bantam, 1972). I follow Ginsburg rather than Guerney in referring to Zamyatin's heroine as 'I-330' not 'E-330'.

2 George Orwell, review of *We* in *Collected Essays, Journalism and Letters*, ed. Sonia Orwell and Ian Angus (London: Secker & Warburg, 1968), IV, pp. 72–75.

3 Mark R. Hillegas, *The Future as Nightmare: H. G. Wells and the Anti-Utopians* (New York: Oxford University Press, 1967), especially pp. 106–09.

utopian may result from the suppression of his works in his native country during the lifetime of the Soviet Union, but it tells us little about the spirit in which *We* was written. In many respects, its author was much closer to Wells than he was to satirists such as Huxley and Orwell.

Zamyatin was an engineer and revolutionary socialist from a remote rural background He studied at the St Petersburg Polytechnic Institute, where he joined the Bolshevik Party. After the 1905 revolution he was imprisoned and exiled, but returned to complete his degree. In 1916, following a further period of political exile, he was sent to England to supervise the construction of ice-breakers for the Tsarist government in the Tyneside shipyards. He returned to Russia in September 1917, and became a leading figure among the left-wing writers of St Petersburg; very soon, however, his outspoken and heretical views came into conflict with the new Soviet government. *We*, his major imaginative work, was banned in the Soviet Union and first published (in 1924) in English translation. Like many of his fellow-writers during the early revolutionary years, Zamyatin was engaged in educational work and in the organisation of state publishing houses. H. G. Wells was one of the first foreign authors to be re-published. (His works had already been widely available under the Tsarist regime, and he visited Russia in 1914 and 1920.) Between 1918 and 1926 Zamyatin edited a new series of Wells translations; at the same time, he wrote *Herbert Wells* (1922), a sparkling survey of the English writer's whole oeuvre. Zamyatin celebrated Wells as the prototype of the modern revolutionary artist, a creator of urban myths who had also pioneered the imaginative exploitation of socialist perspectives. There is little doubt that the author of *We* was setting out to establish himself as Wells's successor.

For Zamyatin, Wells's scientific romances reflected both the endless prospects for technological change and the rigorously logical outlook of scientific culture. They were the fairy-tales of an asphalt-covered, mechanised metropolis, in which the sights and smells of the natural world had been replaced by factory chimneys, test-tubes and motor exhausts. Clearly, it was part of the Russian writer's intention to present Wells as the spokesman of the industrial West— the product of urban landscapes as yet unknown in backward Russia. He believed that Wells's reflection of the twentieth-century environment alone constituted an essential modernity. This side of Wells was summed up in the symbol of the aeroplane, soaring above the given world into a new and unexplored dimension. Just as terrestrial landscape had been transformed by the possibility of aerial photography, so war and revolution were now transforming human prospects. Zamyatin called Wells the most contemporary of writers because he had anticipated this, and taught his readers to see with 'airman's eyes'.[4]

Zamyatin was forced to admit that Wells had come back to earth, however, in the sense of abandoning science fiction for realistic social novels. While suggesting that the social novels were old-fashioned and derivative beside the scientific romances, Zamyatin used the whole range of Wells's writings to support his second theme, that of Wells as a socialist artist. In *Herbert Wells* he quotes passages from Wells's introduction to a Russian edition of his works (1911) in which he declares himself a non-Marxist, non-violent revolutionary—in other words, a heretical socialist like Zamyatin himself.[5] The most surprising twist in the argument is the discussion of Wells's most recent phase, his short-lived conversion to belief in a 'finite God' which was announced in *Mr Britling Sees It Through* in 1916. Wells's wayward attempt to combine rationalism and religion later appeared as an absurdity even to himself; but for Zamyatin it was proof of his independence and imaginative daring. In the aftermath of war, Wells's earlier visions had already come true. 'The whole of life has been torn away from the anchor of reality and has become fantastic', Zamyatin wrote (p. 272). Wells's response had been to pursue his method further, until it touched the ultimate meaning of life. The resulting fusion of socialism and religion was a boldly paradoxical feat recalling the joining of science and myth in the early romances:

> The dry, compass-drawn circle of socialism, limited by the earth, and the hyperbola of religion, stretching into infinity—the two are so different, so incompatible. But Wells managed to breach the circle, bend it into a hyperbola, one end of which rests on the earth, in science and positivism, while the other loses itself in the sky. (p. 273)

Although it made a stir at the time, the spurious religion of *God the Invisible King* and *The Soul of a Bishop* hardly merits this engaging

4 Yevgeny Zamyatin, *Herbert Wells*, trans. Lesley Milne, in Patrick Parrinder, ed., *H. G. Wells: The Critical Heritage* (London and Boston: Routledge & Kegan Paul, 1972), p. 274. Subsequent page references in text.
5 Wells's essay was published in English as 'Mr Wells Explains Himself'.

metaphor. The figure of the circle bent into a hyperbola is associated with the spiralling flight of the aeroplane. Both are found elsewhere in Zamyatin's writings, serving as cryptic images of his theory of art.

In his essay 'On Synthetism' (1922), he divides all art into three schools represented by the mathematical symbols $+$, $-$, $- -$ (affirmation, negation and synthesis). Art develops in a continual dialectical sequence as one school gives way to the next. The three schools in the present phase are naturalism $(+)$, symbolism and futurism $(-)$, and 'neorealism' or 'synthetism'—a post-Cubist and post-Einsteinian art which embraces the paradox of modern experience in being both 'realistic' and 'fantastic'. Characterised by incongruous juxtapositions and the splintering of planes, synthetism is identified in the work of Picasso, Yury Annenkov, Andrey Bely, Alexander Blok and, of course, Zamyatin himself. But this is only a temporary phase, for each dialectical triad is subject to an ongoing process of replacement and succession which observes an eternal oscillation between the extremes of revolution and entropy. Development is a succession of explosions and consolidations, and 'the equation of art is the equation of an infinite spiral'.[6]

These ideas underwrote Zamyatin's commitments to permanent revolution and to the heretical nature of the artist. They are connected to his view of Wells in various ways. In the section of *Herbert Wells* entitled 'Wells's Genealogy', we read that the traditional utopian romance from More to Morris bears a positive sign—the affirmation of a vision of earthly paradise. Wells invents a new form of 'socio-fantastic novel' with a negative sign; its purpose is not the portrayal of a future paradise, but social criticism by extrapolation. There is some ambiguity about these categories, and Zamyatin does not elaborate upon them, but it seems evident that there must also be an anti-utopian form marked $(- -)$. When we follow the struggle of D-503 to achieve mental orthodoxy in *We*, and more fleetingly as we contemplate the brainwashed Winston Smith at the end of Orwell's *Nineteen Eighty-Four*, the impossibility of our imagining such a future at all—in any full sense—is what the author confronts us with. Is this perhaps the negation of the negation?

Such reasoning would limit Wells to an intermediate place in the dialectic of anti-utopia. Zamyatin usually sees him in a more general

6 Yevgeny Zamyatin, 'On Synthetism', in *A Soviet Heretic: Essays*, ed. Mirra Ginsburg (Chicago and London: University of Chicago Press, 1970), p. 82.

way as a symbol of the dynamism of the contemporary imagination. The aeroplane spiralling upwards from the earth is not just Wells but a figure for contemporary writing as a whole.[7] Moreover, Wells's success as a prophet of change confirmed his position as a vanguard artist, and indeed as a 'neorealist'. Destroying the stable picture of Victorian society with his strange, forward-looking logic, he had foreseen the revolutionary age when reality would itself become fantastic. Zamyatin credited him with the invention of a type of fable reflecting the demands of modern experience—speed, logic, the unforeseen. Yet for all this there was one area in which he lagged behind: 'language, style, the word—all those things that we have come to appreciate in the most recent Russian writers'.[8] One of Zamyatin's metaphors for art is 'a winding staircase in the Tower of Babel'.[9] He heralded a verbal and syntactic revolution generating language that was 'supercharged, high-voltage'[10], and he set out to create such a language in the writing of *We*. To pass from the Wellsian prophetic romances to *We* is to enter a future world where the topography may be similar, but the nature of experience has utterly changed; so that we are faced with two quite different kinds of imagination.

II

We takes the form of a diary. It is true that D-503, the diarist, makes some conscientious attempts to explain his society to alien readers, but the social picture which emerges (the sole concern of an ideologically-minded critic such as Orwell) is revealed through the medium of the future consciousness—and the future language— which are Zamyatin's most radical conceptions. The reflection that a new society entails new consciousness and language, and that these can only be adequately suggested by a 'futuristic' fictional technique, seems obvious once stated. Yet it is Zamyatin's imagination of these conditions, his revelation of the future through a new mode of writing and thinking, that establishes *We* as a uniquely modernist work of science fiction.

J. Hillis Miller has observed that 'the transformation which makes

7 See for example Yevgeny Zamyatin, 'On Literature, Revolution, Entropy, and Other Matters' in *A Soviet Heretic*, pp. 107–12.

8 Yevgeny Zamyatin, *Herbert Wells*, pp. 268–69.

9 Yevgeny Zamyatin, 'On Synthetism', p. 81.

10 Yevgeny Zamyatin, 'On Literature, Revolution, Entropy', p. 111.

a man a novelist is his decision to adopt the role of the narrator who tells the story'.[11] The contrast between Wells's influential model of the science-fiction fable and the form that Zamyatin created is, above all, due to the difference in the role of the narrator. In *Herbert Wells*, Zamyatin refers to the English writer's 'strange gift of prophecy' as a 'gift for seeing the future through the opaque curtain of the present' (p. 262). He sees the future like an 'aviator' (p. 272). Implicitly, these metaphors suggest a vision of vague, even shadowy forms seen from a distance and through an intervening medium such as the curtain or the pilot's windscreen and goggles. The Wellsian narrator faces the unknown—but Zamyatin's narrator is the unknown. For all their power of prophetic revelation, Wells's narratives retain a fixed and familiar point of reference. Like the philosophical tales of Swift and Voltaire, they exploit the Enlightenment forms of the travelogue and the scientific report. In his early romances there is always a narrator who brings weird and disturbing news and yet wins our confidence at once by his observance of anecdotal conventions. His audience is either today's audience or that of the very near future, and his assumptions are those of contemporary scientific culture.

In *The Time Machine*, the Traveller sets out armed with expectant curiosity, quick wits and a cheerful acceptance of danger—the very type of the gentleman-explorer. In the Epilogue, however, we are casually told that he 'thought but cheerlessly of the Advancement of Mankind' even before he began on his journey. The information is held back so that nothing shall interfere with his confidence in the value of knowing the future. Similarly, in *The Island of Doctor Moreau*, Prendick is a rational, eye-witness observer who only emerges as insanely misanthropic in the final pages. By such concealments the potential displacement of the whole narrative is avoided. In *The War of the Worlds* we are told at the outset that the humanist conception of the universe has been shattered by the Martian invasion, but the narrator addresses us in the established terms of rational discourse, and then reassures us of his own essential normality: 'For my own part, I was much occupied in learning to ride the bicycle, and busy upon a series of papers discussing the probable developments of moral ideas as civilisation progressed' (I, 1). In each case, what is portrayed is a biological and an anthropological endeavour; the book

11 J. Hillis Miller, *The Form of Victorian Fiction* (Notre Dame and London: University of Notre Dame Press, 1968), p. 62.

is an exposition both of an alien society and of the attempts of a representative bourgeois observer to know it empirically (hence the importance of the narrator's observation of the Martians from the ruined house, a literal 'camera obscura'). The narrator in *The War of the Worlds* is drawn to the Martians, though he does not reject human norms as completely as Gulliver and Prendick do. Both Swift and Wells recognised the potential destructiveness of the scientific spirit. Wells's attempt to play down this perception appears more deliberate than Swift's insofar as he is making a self-consciously literary choice of narrative forms deriving from the eighteenth-century; prophecy and parody thus go together.

In later romances Wells dropped the rational observer in favour of characters who participate directly in the alien world. Unfortunately, the usual result is the cruder and less exacting form of adventure narrative typified by *When the Sleeper Wakes*. There are a number of significant experiments with a split narrative, such as *The First Men in the Moon* and *A Modern Utopia*, or with a self-divided autobiographical narrator, as in *Tono-Bungay*. Nevertheless, in science fiction the Wellsian model remained an adaptation of Enlightenment narrative forms based on the literature of travel and reportage.

The effect of moving from Wells's romances to *We* might be compared to the experience of Zamyatin's narrator as he passes beyond the Green Wall of the city:

> It was then I opened my eyes—and was face to face, in reality, with that very sort of thing which up to then none of those living had seen other than diminished a thousand times, weakened, smudged over by the turbid glass of the Wall.
>
> The sun—it was no longer that sun of ours, proportionately distributed over the mirror-like surface of the pavements; this sun consisted of some sort of living splinters of incessantly bobbing spots which blinded one's eyes, made one's head go round. And the trees—like candles thrusting into the very sky, like spiders squatting flat against the earth on their gnarled paws, like mute fountains jetting green . . .
> (pp. 192–93)

This is a new reality, neither seen through a glass (a recurrent mode of vision in Wells), nor in the even light of scientific reasonableness. Experience is splintered and blinding; the head whirls and the self loses its centre of gravity. The writer is at the mercy of disparate

impressions, and merely records his conflicting impulses as they
mount to a nauseous intensity. Although he tries to control his
unruly consciousness by a 'rational' method, it is the method of a
society not our own.

III

We begins with a directive inviting all 'numbers' (citizens) to com-
pose poems or treatises celebrating the One State, to be carried on
the first flight of the space-rocket Integral as an aid to subjugating the
people of other planets. To the narrator, D-503 (the builder of the
Integral), this is a divine command, but to the reader the forcing of a
'mathematically infallible happiness' (p. 23) upon unknown peoples
is brutally imperialistic. The value of space travel itself is thus called
into question (a very un-Wellsian touch), by means of the ironical
device of a narrator who worships mathematical exactitude and
straight lines. Yet as soon as the alienness of D-503's outlook has
been established, it becomes clear that he himself is internally torn.
He undertakes literary composition as a duty to the state, but chooses
to write, not a poem in accordance with the approved, public literary
genres (the poetry of the One State is about as rich and varied as that
of Swift's Houyhnhnms), but a simple record of his day-to-day
impressions. The conflict of group and private consciousness signi-
fied by the novel's title is thus outlined by his initial choice of mode of
writing; he thinks to express what 'We' experience, but his record
becomes irretrievably subjective. Already as he begins his diary his
'cheeks are flaming' and he feels as though a child stirred inside him
(p. 24)—dangerous signs, for the irrationality of sensation and of the
philoprogenitive emotion are motifs of rebellion throughout the
novel (O-90's longing for a child parallels D-503's creative instinct,
and during the brief revolutionary outbreak in the One State couples
are seen shamelessly copulating in the public view.) As he writes his
diary, D-503 becomes increasingly conscious of the lack of continuity in his thoughts and the disruption of logical processes. Finally
he goes to the doctors, who diagnose the diseased growth known as a
soul. A healthy consciousness, he is told, is simply a reflecting
medium like a mirror; but he has developed an absorptive capacity,
an inner dimension which retains and memorises. The disease
becomes epidemic in the State, and universal fantasiectomy is
ordained to wipe it out. Superficially D-503 develops a soul as a
result of falling in love with the fascinating I-330, but really it is
constituted by the act of writing. It is his identity as a man who

wishes to write down his sensations that throws him into mental crisis. And it is the diary that betrays him, together with his rebellious accomplices, to the secret police.

It may seem that the one error of the 'mathematically perfect State' was to encourage its members to engage in literary expression at all—as in Ray Bradbury's *Fahrenheit 451*, things might run more smoothly if all the books were burnt. On the other hand, perhaps D-503 has fallen into a cunningly set trap. In the end the rebellion is crushed, D-503 undergoes fantasiectomy, and he watches the public torturing of I-330, sensible only of the aesthetic beauty of the spectacle. Notwithstanding our reaction, from the viewpoint of the State his story seems to be an exemplary cautionary tale. We cannot be sure about this, because Zamyatin implies the ultimate inexpressibility of his future society—its experience and culture are structured in ways which remain somewhat mysterious. The narrator tries to explain things for the benefit of alien peoples stuck at a twentieth-century level of development, but he also feels like a geometrical square charged to explain its existence to human beings: 'The last thing that would enter this quadrangle's mind, you understand, would be to say that all its four angles are equal' (p. 46). A similar argument may apply to the status of the book itself.

The classic satirical utopia establishes a social picture through incongruous comparisons, and *We* does this too: for example, the work of ancient literature most treasured in its future society is the railway timetable. But Zamyatin suggests a more disturbing and bewildering alienness than this method can convey. A new experience is rendered in an unprecedented language or languages, for D-503's diary is a theatre of dialogical conflict. His orthodox selfhood is expressed through a logical discourse, syllogistic in form and drawing repeatedly on mathematics, geometry and engineering for its stock of metaphors. (There are obvious resemblances to the aggressively 'technocratic' style of Zamyatin's essays.) This is the language in which citizens of the One State are trained to reconstruct the infallible reasoning behind the state's bald directives. Even women's faces are analysed in terms of geometrical figures, circles and triangles. But this orthodox, mathematical language is unable to subdue the whole of D-503's experience. He may see his brain as a machine, but it is an overheated machine which vaporises the coolant of logic. He becomes uncomfortably self-conscious, and his mental operations are no longer smooth and automatic. His analysis of I-330's face reveals two acute triangles forming an 'X'—the algebraic symbol of the unknown. More unknowns supervene, and his memory is forced back to the symbol of unreason in the very foundations of the mathematics he was taught at school: $\sqrt{-1}$, the square root of minus one. Soon he confronts the existence of a whole universe of irrationals, of $\sqrt{-1}$ solids lurking in the non-Euclidean space of subjective experience. To his diseased mind, mathematics, the basis of his society, seems divided against itself.

The 'X' or unknown element in *We* always arises within personal experience. It is identified first in the meeting with I-330, and we sense it in the quality of their dialogue—probing, spontaneous and electric—which contrasts sharply with the formulaic responses of the narrator's orthodox discourse. He has been taught to reduce everything to a mathematicised environment, but as soon as he describes impressions and people, his account takes on an acutely nervous vitality. As the diary proceeds, the hegemony of orthodox discourse diminishes, and the 'splintered' style of *We* is established— the shifting, expressionistic movement of thought which is the basic experience of Zamyatin's reader. The narrator's mood and attention are volatile and constantly changing, sensations are momentary, and thoughts, whether 'correct' or heretical, are only provisional. Utterances are characteristically left unfinished. Torn by the confusion of this kaleidoscopic language, D-503 struggles to maintain his conviction that self-expression will somehow lead to eventual order and clarification. Yet in fact it leads to the consciousness of a schizoid identity, from which only fantasiectomy can rescue him.

We does describe a revolution in the streets, but the narrator's involvement is confused and accidental, for the real battleground is within his head. The languages involved are futuristic, and (with some lapses) the fixed points to which D-503 can refer are different from ours. Moreover, once his experience has transcended the limitations for which he has been programmed, he is unable to make elementary distinctions between dream and reality. Zamyatin's decision to abandon any outside narrative viewpoint and to enter the unknowns of consciousness, not merely those of politics and technology, makes *We* one of the most remarkable science fictions of the twentieth century.

IV

'A literature that is alive', Zamyatin wrote, 'does not live by yesterday's clock, nor by today's but by tomorrow's'. 'What we need in literature today are vast philosophic horizons—horizons seen from mastheads, from airplanes; we need the most ultimate, the most fearsome, the most fearless "Why?" and "What next?" '[12] The author of *We* had earned the right to make such exacting demands, but in subsequent science fiction and futuristic fiction, including Wells's later writings in the genre, they are but feebly met. The language of most modern science fiction differs very little from the language of realism or of other kinds of popular romance and adventure fiction. Where the basic assumptions of story and characterisation remain unchanged, a limited amount of verbal innovation is, at best, a sort of mannerism. Ivan Yefremov, author of the popular Soviet space-tale *Andromeda*, outlined a typical attitude:

> The mass of scientific information and intricate terminology used in the story are the result of a deliberate plan. It seemed to me that this is the only way to show our distant descendants and give the necessary local (or temporal) colour to their dialogue since they are living in a period when science will have penetrated into all human conceptions and into language itself.[13]

All that is promised here is 'local colour'—which Yefremov achieves by inserting scientific jargon into the conventional emotive situations of sentimental fiction. If Yefremov's attitude is the norm, there have been some distinguished attempts since Zamyatin's to create the experience and consciousness of an alien culture through altered or alienated language. William Golding's *The Inheritors* (1955) is a notable example—and Golding, like Zamyatin, was both extending and repudiating the Wellsian legacy. Much more representative, however, is the case of the one English novel which transmits Zamyatin's direct influence, Orwell's *Nineteen Eighty-Four*.

What Orwell as an artist responds to in Zamyatin is not merely his ideological critique of the totalitarian state and his understanding of its paranoid ruthlessness, but his skill as a parodist. The excerpt from the *One State Gazette* with which D-503 begins his diary provides a model for the numerous slogans and public proclamations recorded in *Nineteen Eighty-Four*. The use of the diary as a narrative device, however, is very different in the two novels. Winston's diary, which

12 Yevgeny Zamyatin, 'On Literature, Revolution, Entropy', pp. 109–10.

13 Ivan Yefremov, *Andromeda: A Space-Age Tale* (Moscow, 1959), dust-jacket quotation.

is inserted into a conventional third-person narrative, is an intermittent and strictly limited outlet for his rebellious thoughts. After the first entries, written when he was 'seized by a kind of hysteria',[14] he no longer seems to be discovering his feelings in the act of writing them, as D-503 continually does. Winston's activities as a writer and as a rebel are easily distinguishable.

Orwell gives us, in many respects, a sardonic English humorist's response to Zamyatin. The One State's sanitised moral permissiveness, with its Sexual Days and issues of pink tickets, turns into the puritanical repression of the Junior Anti-Sex League. Instead of ' "All hail to The Benefactor" ' we have ' "Big Brother is Watching You" '. Orwell's most futuristic conception, however, is Newspeak, a satire on modern propaganda techniques and also on rational language schemes such as Basic English. Yet Newspeak is only the public rhetoric of Oceania, it is relegated to an Appendix in the novel, and it is not scheduled for final adoption until 2050. Winston Smith still thinks and speaks in Standard English. *Nineteen Eighty-Four* may thus be regarded as a domestication of the rootless, modernist technique of *We*—a prophetic satire grounded in the tradition of English realism and in the London landscape that Orwell knew, with an appended vision of linguistic change. For the last half-century Orwell's reputation, not those of Wells or Zamyatin, has been something to conjure with. Yet *Nineteen Eighty-Four* may well turn out to be the sort of futuristic writing which, as Wells put it, has little prospect of becoming permanent literature.[15] Whatever its merits as a political novel and a psychological thriller, Orwell's book is at its weakest (where *We* is at its strongest) considered as a science-fictional work. It is Zamyatin, not Orwell, who deserves to be studied by future science-fiction writers.

14 George Orwell, *Nineteen Eighty-Four* (Harmondsworth: Penguin, 1954), p. 19.
15 H. G. Wells, 'Utopias', p. 117.

CHAPTER NINE
From Prophecy to Parody: Science Fiction and the Scientific Enlightenment

I

The problems of writing about the relationship between science and science fiction are manifold. It is necessary not only to define one's terms but to dispel a widespread suspicion that the relationship is accidental rather than essential. Do the initials 'SF' have to stand for *science* fiction? Many have wished that they didn't. One could compile an anthology of dismissing or patronising references to science fiction by practising scientists (though Arthur C. Clarke has suggested that they might mostly be second-rate scientists).[1] A much livelier anthology would display science-fiction writers, particularly recent ones, pouring scorn on the idea that their work has anything to do with institutionalised knowledge. 'Like most science-fiction writers', Kurt Vonnegut says of his protagonist Kilgore Trout, 'Trout knew almost nothing about science, was bored stiff by technical details'.[2] And Brian Aldiss once asserted that 'Most of science fiction is about as firmly based in science as eggs are filled with bacon'.[3]

One could answer these statements by saying that they are demonstrably untrue: there are probably very few significant developments in modern physics, astronomy, cybernetics, biology and genetics—to go no further—which have not been reflected in science-fiction stories. Equally, the denial of any connection between science fiction and science is a species of deliberate heresy.

---

1 Arthur C. Clarke, *Profiles of the Future: An Enquiry into the Limits of the Possible* (London: Gollancz, 1962), pp. 10–11.

2 Kurt Vonnegut, Jr., *Breakfast of Champions* (New York: Delta, 1973), p. 123.

3 Brian Aldiss, *The Shape of Further Things: Speculation on Change* (London: Corgi, 1974), p. 127.

For many years SF writers in England and America formed a largely ingrown community, cut off from the mainstream of literary culture by their outspoken support for the values of scientists and technologists. By the 1960s there was an understandable desire to break out of the ghetto and assert the continuity between SF and other forms of contemporary fiction. At the same time, there was a loss of confidence in the scientific world-view which had inspired so many writers of earlier decades. The period of ascendancy of scientific materialism—an ideology justifying scientific research as intrinsic to the meaning and purpose of human existence—began with the technological triumphs and erosion of traditional religious beliefs caused by the Industrial Revolution. The growth of science fiction as a separate genre would be unthinkable without this ascendancy.

Hugo Gernsback, who is often regarded as the inventor of genre science fiction, introduced the first number of his magazine *Science Wonder Stories* (June 1929) with the declaration that it was the magazine's policy to 'publish only such stories that have their basis in scientific laws as we know them, or in the logical deduction of new laws from what we know'. At the same time, he announced that he was enlisting a panel of experts to pronounce on the scientific correctness of stories submitted to the magazine.[4] Three years earlier Gernsback had coined the term 'scientifiction', defining it as follows: 'By "scientifiction" I mean the Jules Verne, H. G. Wells, and Edgar Allan Poe type of story—a charming romance intermingled with scientific fact and prophetic vision'.[5] Within this generic mixture it may be argued that it was the prophetic vision of science-fiction writers, much more than their correctness in matters of detail, which reflected their general imaginative debt to scientific ideology. This ideology has often received its fullest expression in stories, such as those concerning time travel, which at some point flagrantly violate 'scientific fact'.

Mary Shelley's *Frankenstein* (1818) would undoubtedly have been thrown out by the *Science Wonder Stories* panel of scientific experts. Yet this is one of the earliest science-fiction novels because it takes us into the laboratory and shows the horrifying results of a scientist's

4 See Paul A. Carter, *The Creation of Tomorrow* (New York: Columbia University Press, 1977), p. 11.

5 Quoted in Gary Westfahl, ' "The Jules Verne, H. G. Wells, and Edgar Allan Poe Type of Story": Hugo Gernsback's History of Science Fiction', *Science-Fiction Studies* 58 (November 1992), p. 342.

researches into the principles of life. Victor Frankenstein creates life by collecting the materials of a human body from dissecting-rooms and slaughterhouses, and then galvanising the creature with the 'vital spark' of electricity. The power of electricity is suggested by the thunderstorms which crackle through the novel, as well as by the blackened lips and shrivelled skin of the hideous creature itself. Science, in this Gothic melodrama, stands accused of perverting the awesome power of natural forces to ungodly ends. Frankenstein's researches do irreparable damage to himself and his family, and his last words are a warning against the ambition of distinguishing oneself in science and discoveries.

The isolated, demonic inventor remains a classic figure of 'scientific romance', but the development of the genre throughout the nineteenth century reflects the steady institutionalisation of science, as uncoordinated 'discoveries' and 'inventions' gave way to organised programmes of education and research. Jules Verne's romances have a strong element of scientific education without tears. H. G. Wells began by writing textbooks of biology and physiography, and several of his early novels were reviewed in the scientific periodical *Nature* as well as in more conventional journals. The widespread foundation of learned societies, professional journals, laboratories and university courses during the Victorian period conferred on the 'scientist' or 'specialist' (the words were coined in 1840 and 1856 respectively) a growing degree of public esteem. What T. H. Huxley called the 'ethical spirit' of science, sceptical, experimental and rigorously impersonal, had a wide impact on social thought, literature and the arts. Science and technology held the key to 'progress' and thus represented bourgeois society's investment in its own future.

Scientific thought has most influenced science fiction where it has itself contained a strong vein of prophetic fantasy. The prospects of space travel and evolution beyond man have played an important part in this. Space travel is an age-old dream which appealed to the Victorian rationalist as representing the final goal of human progress. Thus Winwood Reade's *The Martyrdom of Man* (1872), a Positivist account of human history which remained in print for fifty years and was still selling in its tens of thousands in the 1920s, looks forward to a time when disease has been extirpated, immortality has been 'invented' and human beings have migrated into space. 'The earth will become a Holy Land', Reade predicts, 'which will be visited by pilgrims from all quarters of the universe'.[6] Finally, mankind will master the forces of nature and will set out to build new universes. Reade's 'religion of humanity' was very obviously modelled on the Christian religion, with scientists eventually usurping the function of God. Such perspectives were ridiculed by more sober-minded scientific observers, including Huxley whose lecture 'On the Advisableness of Improving Natural Knowledge' (1860) dismisses the idea of science as a fairy godmother bringing 'omnipotent Aladdin's lamps' and 'telegraphs to Saturn'.[7] In the early twentieth century, however, the invention of powered flight made space travel no longer seem an absurdity. The discovery of radioactivity promised to unleash a source of unlimited energy. Meanwhile, developments in biology led not only to the control of ageing and disease but to the prospect of a planned 'improvement' of the human race by means of genetic engineering. Yet it was not until the 1920s that there emerged a coherent body of thought bringing together all the elements of the future vision that we have learned to call 'science-fictional'. It is in this body of popular scientific thought, and most notably in works by Wells, J. B. S. Haldane and J. D. Bernal, that we may find the most significant link between scientific materialism and modern science fiction.

The reasons why this futurological perspective or 'Scientific Enlightenment' took coherent shape when and where it did are highly complex, and only a few suggestions can be made here. Modern scientific optimism reached its peak in the 1920s as a reaction against the traditionalist thinking which was thought to have caused the First World War. Although an international movement, it received its most authoritative intellectual statement in Europe, and especially Britain, while in the United States it was most fully represented by Gernsback and his successors in the science-fiction magazines. It has often been suggested that the Scientific Enlightenment was the ideology of a new class of engineers and technical experts, a sector of the petty-bourgeoisie who hoped to gain enormously in power and influence as the planned society that they foresaw came about. Wells saw himself as the prophet of an 'Open Conspiracy' of scientists, technicians and industrialists who

6 Winwood Reade, *The Martyrdom of Man* (London: Watts, 1924), p. 423.

7 Thomas H. Huxley, 'On the Advisableness of Improving Natural Knowledge' (1860), in *Methods and Results: Essays* (London: Macmillan, 1904), p. 30.

would take over world government, while both Haldane and Bernal were advocates of the combination of collectivism and the high status of the specialist that they found in the Soviet Union.

In Britain and Europe the vision of a scientific, collectivist future was in sharp contrast to the established or (in Russia) the recently destroyed social structure. The United States, however, was seen as an inherently dynamic, wealth-creating society which already represented 'the future'. In America technological developments were more immediately put in the service of consumer-oriented capitalism than in Europe, where the first priority was often national defence. It may have been for these reasons that the most influential American proponents of scientific materialism expressed a much narrower and more manipulative attitude than their European counterparts. Pragmatism, the philosophy of 'if it works, it's right' originating in the thought of C. S. Peirce and William James, prepared the ground for the techniques of 'social engineering' advocated by F. W. Taylor in *The Principles of Scientific Management* (1911), and later by the behaviourist school of psychology. The aim of social engineering is to increase efficiency by modernising all aspects of industrial production. Its range thus extends from the time-and-motion study advocated by Taylor (and satirised in Zamyatin's *We*) to the social welfare programmes of the New Deal in the 1930s. The extension of 'scientific management' into the control of all human behaviour is envisaged in B. F. Skinner's utopian novel *Walden Two* (1948), which portrays a perfect community set up within the existing capitalist system. Skinner's behaviourism holds that human fulfilment can be attained as a result of psychological techniques to be applied, without any structural or political change, in the here and now.

After the Second World War, the development of nuclear arsenals and the Cold War between East and West produced a new phase of American technological materialism. Technical innovations and scientific progress were now the secret weapon in America's struggle to hold on to the dominance it had acquired in the battlegrounds of Europe and the Far East. The 'space race' was a reflection of superpower rivalry, not of the united human effort for which Wells and his successors had called. The establishment of 'futurology' as a branch of social science was fatally compromised by its association with the cold-blooded perspectives of military strategists such as Herman Kahn. The therapeutic perspective of a bestselling book like Alvin Toffler's *Future Shock* (1970) reflects the dehumanisation of scientific progress, as something imposed by national economic imperatives irrespective of the social or political will. Toffler is concerned not with the desirable directions of change as such, but with ways of softening the impact of uncontrolled change on the individual. This tendency to concentrate on the individual psyche as the key social unit was shared by advocates of behavioural engineering on the one hand, and by anti-rationalists and neo-mystics on the other.

II

The scientific materialism of Wells, Haldane, Bernal and their successors has at its centre neither dehumanised technological rationality nor the atomised individual but the entity 'man': man considered not as a divinely created being or a paragon of reason, but as a competing biological species. Today, partly as a result of feminist critique, this use of 'man' as a generic term (and with it an intellectual tradition stretching from the Renaissance to the twentieth century) has been widely questioned. It is true that a degree of conceptual slippage was widespread in the Scientific Enlightenment, though not usually from 'man' to 'male human being' as is frequently alleged. Instead, 'man' became 'civilised man' and, in effect, 'modern Western man', with modernity being equated with the capacity to pursue scientific research. Scientific pronouncements about 'man's survival' tended to reflect the interests of the social groups to which the scientists belonged. Typically, they looked to action by world bodies such as the United Nations (or its predecessor the League of Nations) to bring about the changes which were desired. The League of Nations idea of joint action by governments to ensure peace and mutual security reflected an idealism which arose out of the carnage of the First World War, but which also suggested a desire to stave off the 'anarchy' of revolutions like that which had taken place in Russia. The common interest of 'mankind' was taken for granted by some (if not all) of the scientific thinkers of the 1920s and 1930s. Their articulation of the problems and prospects confronting 'man'—an articulation largely present in Wells, and yet considerably extended by his successors, including some science-fiction writers—may be loosely sketched as follows:

1. The immediate challenge to mankind is the self-destructiveness inherent in the present phase of social and technological evolution. The nightmare of technological warfare, as foreseen by Wells and

other futuristic novelists, was unleashed in the Great War of 1914–18. Future wars, it is anticipated, will be world wars, destructive of civilisation as a whole. War has become irrational because no one side stands any longer to gain by it. If major wars are to be avoided, the advanced societies must learn to control their own 'inner demons' and those of others. Such control is to be achieved by a framework of international legal and political coordination, by the spread of education and the use of social engineering (i.e. social reform directed from above) to remove poverty and injustice—the source of the frustrations and inequalities which breed demagogy and mass hysteria—and by the transfer of power to a scientific élite.

2. It is when it looks beyond the horizons of the immediate crisis that scientific thinking enters the eschatological dimension which is the territory of much science fiction. Once the problems of war, poverty, frustration and ignorance have been overcome, what is to come next? From an evolutionary point of view, humanity would be free to apply the principles of social engineering at will to its own further development. Since there is no finality in the evolutionary process—except that of extinction—we cannot look to the stabilisation or conservation of any features of our present civilisation as a long-term goal. The aim, accordingly, must be to transcend our present cultural, and eventually biological, identity. The vision of 'evolution beyond man' is usually presented by some grotesque marriage of biology and cybernetics; the inheritors of human civilisation will be either organisms with vastly distended brains (as in Wells and Stapledon) or computers which have liberated themselves from their human constructors. The first steps toward further development will be taken as human beings learn to inhabit wholly artificial environments, to consume artificial foods and adopt artificial means of reproduction and the prolongation of life.

3. As consolation for this loss of natural life there is the last and greatest of the physical challenges that humanity faces: the conquest of space. Once the gospel of a small number of writers and thinkers mocked by the public at large, space research has become both an economic and military reality and one of the staple components of mass-entertainment fantasy.

  While the practicability of star travel awaits the discovery of some mode of faster-than-light propulsion, travel within the solar system depends upon simple extensions of the transport technology which has produced the motor-car and the jet aeroplane. The mid-twentieth-century revolution in attitudes to space is vividly recorded in the files of periodicals like the *Journal of the British Interplanetary Society*, founded in 1934 by a small group of visionaries, which by the late 1940s had become a professional journal for rocket engineers, most of whom were employed on government-assisted research projects. Writing in the *Journal* for December 1946, Arthur C. Clarke recalled that in *Possible Worlds* (1927) J. B. S. Haldane had predicted space travel around the year 8 million. Now, Clarke suggested a little too optimistically, there was a possibility of a guided missile crashing on to the moon by 1950![8] For decades before this, however, scientific thinkers and science-fiction writers had discussed the possibilities of colonising neighbouring planets, the exploitation of mineral resources and the sale of real estate on them, and the likelihood of discovering alien life-forms. 'Space' had become a new frontier of the imagination, at once the last repository of the colonist's dream of a clean break and a new start, and the ultimate target of capitalism's drive towards perpetual expansion.

Beyond the practical advantages of opening up the solar system, space travel has always had a quasi-religious attraction for certain minds. Winwood Reade's *The Martyrdom of Man* has already been cited as an example of this, and Wells is perhaps the most important writer to echo the strain of religious exaltation in which Reade had written of space. In *The Discovery of the Future* Wells looks forward to a time when 'beings who are now latent in our thoughts and hidden in our loins, shall stand upon this earth as one stands upon a footstool, and shall laugh and reach out their hands amid the stars' (p. 36). Like the universe makers prophesied by Reade, these human children who take the heavens for their playground are substitutes for the traditional gods.

In the long term there is a more sombre reason for embarking on space travel, which scientific thinkers have seldom failed to point out. The time will come (though maybe not for millions of years) when the earth will no longer be able to support human life. Whether as a result of the planet's natural cooling or of some purely man-made disaster, enforced migration will become the key to survival. The certainty that humankind, having survived the most immediate dangers, must one day face the choice of leaving the earth

8 Arthur C. Clarke, 'The Challenge of the Spaceship', *Journal of the British Interplanetary Society* 6:3 (December 1946), p. 69.

or becoming extinct makes space travel appear as a form of positive evolutionary adaptation. Space is of the essence of the Scientific Enlightenment, for it represents not only 'man's' future playground but his destiny.

4. After reading Wells, Lenin is reported to have said that 'If we could enter into interplanetary contacts, we would have to revise all our philosophic, social and moral notions; in that case, the technological possibilities would become limitless and would put an end to violence as means and method of progress'.[9] While statistical probability seems to support the inference that there is or has been intelligent life elsewhere in the universe, there is no doubt that scientific materialists have by and large *wanted* to believe this. In the 1890s popular astronomy championed the idea that intelligent beings must have constructed the newly discovered 'canals' on Mars. Now that we no longer expect to encounter a rival civilisation anywhere in the solar system, speculation centres on the possibility of establishing a communications network across interstellar space. The astronomer Fred Hoyle has written that, while travel outside the solar system may be 'not merely difficult but impossible', the rate of information-exchange may be such that we could stumble across a 'galactic library' and a 'galactic telephone directory'. In this way we might even profit from the experience of other civilisations which have learned to avoid nuclear war![10] Similarly, many science-fiction writers have imagined extraterrestrials arriving out of the blue and establishing a benevolent despotism—a sort of intergalactic Open Conspiracy—to save mankind from its follies. Against this, Arthur C. Clarke suggested in 1951 that although the chances of intelligence existing elsewhere in the universe are very high, the probability of our encountering a civilisation at a stage of development recognisably close to our own is infinitesimal. In 1993 the United States Senate voted to terminate a $12 million-a-year government project using large radiotelescopes directed at the stars in the hope of picking up signals and messages. But even if contact with other civilisations turns out to be a purely fictional prospect, the doubt whether human intelligence is alone in the universe does much to mitigate the bleakness of scientific cosmology.

9 Cited by E. Drabkina, 'Memories of Lenin', *Izvestiia*, 22 December 1961. I am indebted to Darko Suvin for this information.

10 Fred Hoyle, *Of Men and Galaxies* (London: Heinemann, 1965), pp. 41, 47.

5. Modern scientific thought places humankind in a time and space so large as to annihilate the individual with a normal human life-span. The inherently anti-individualistic quality of the evolutionary outlook has constituted one of its most powerful attractions. Scientific thinkers such as Wells, Haldane and Bernal reject the 'short-sighted' materialistic and pragmatic goals of modern democracies in favour of a more self-sacrificing concern for the welfare of the species as a whole. It may be that in rejecting individualism, more fundamentally than in its dreams of space travel, artificial environments and alien intelligence, the Scientific Enlightenment reflects some of the deeper and as yet unsatisfied yearnings of human culture.

The 'spiritual' goal of the evolutionary process, according to Wells and his successors, is some sort of collective mind or intelligence incorporating the whole human race. Such a collective mind is a materialisation of a metaphorical idea which already exists; phrases such as 'collective mind' and 'collective wisdom' have a long history. Wells gave to a book arguing for an integrated, world-wide information service the title *World Brain* (1938), and the contemporary form of a world brain is the information superhighway or Internet. Nevertheless, the realisation of a collective mind in the full sense implies the attainment of an unprecedented harmony between the minds of individuals. Such a prospect may have authoritarian or liberal overtones; indeed, the mixture of individual subordination and fraternal intimacy that it involves might be said to exist at the vanishing-point where 'total democracy' equals 'totalitarianism'. As long as the harmony that is attained is founded on the recognition of scientific truths, the achievement of a state of collective mind is, according to Wells, the ultimate goal of science itself.

Science fiction, as a genre, is not devoted to collectivism. Some of its best-known writers, such as Robert A. Heinlein, are right-wing individualists whose heroes stand out by virtue of their individual courage, expertise and contempt for the herd. Nevertheless, science fiction has repeatedly given expression to the dream of mental harmony, most strikingly in its use of themes of telepathy or 'mindspeech'. Whether brought about by a form of religious discipline (as in Ursula K. Le Guin's novels) or by the simple electronic expedient of connecting two brains together (as envisaged by J. D. Bernal), telepathy may be looked upon as a form of biological mutation which would release us from the prison of our individuality. A sharp distinction should be drawn here between science fiction which portrays telepathy as a further stage of human development, as most memorably in Olaf Stapledon's *Last and First Men*, and the mass of fantasies which make it magically available to selected characters in today's world. Where they are not put in the service of sheer escapism, telepathy and 'psi' powers can be one of the most subversive elements in the outlook of scientific materialism. The idea of a collective mind not only involves a radical evolution in the biological nature of intelligence; it may be one of the science's most far-reaching contributions to the dream of human brotherhood.

III

Though enormously influential in its day, Wells's championship of scientific materialism is now enshrined for the most part in little-read books, written after the completion of his major science-fiction cycle around the turn of the century. The concept of collective mind, for example, was introduced in *First and Last Things* (a book which went through several revisions), and finally elaborated in the DSc thesis that he completed in 1944, two years before his death. The development of new social structures and the emergence of world government are the principal concerns of his political thought. Other themes, such as space travel, alien intelligence and the detailed projection of further biological evolution, belong much more to his science fiction. It was the combination in Wells of the visionary and the untiring propagandist that made him recognised by his contemporaries as the representative spokesman of the Scientific Enlightenment.

Although the movement had its roots in Positivist philosophy and the science-versus-religion debates of the nineteenth century, its rhetoric took account of newer developments such as pragmatism, logical positivism and the growth of a specialised philosophy of science. By the early twentieth century scientists were accustomed to appeal to the scientific 'attitude' or 'method', rather than to 'facts' and 'laws' as their predecessors had done. Measured by this yardstick all sorts of social practices, from metaphysics to ornamental architecture and slum housing, were found wanting. Science was seen as a progressive, subversive and destabilising influence on society. As late as 1959 C. P. Snow could plausibly affirm that, statistically, 'more scientists [were] on the left in open politics', and that, whether left or right, they had 'the future in their bones'.[11] In the 1940s and

11 C. P. Snow, *The Two Cultures: and A Second Look* (New York: Mentor, 1964), p. 16.

1950s Snow's statistical majority of left-inclined scientists included most of the world-famous leaders of the profession, as well as numbers of popular science writers and journalists. Some, like Bernal and J. F. Joliot-Curie, were pillars of the world Communist movement. Other left-wing scientists criticised Communism in its Stalinist guise as not being scientific enough. Gary Werskey in his history of scientists in the 1930s has argued that, even for a Marxist like Bernal, science was a transcendent force acting as the prime mover of human history.[12] Similarly, the liberal C. H. Waddington in his popular exposition of *The Scientific Attitude* (1941) asserted that science itself was a crucial source of political values. Science, Waddington wrote, 'has certain social requirements on whose satisfaction it must insist'.[13]

In Britain the Scientific Enlightenment reached its apogee in the late 1930s, as can be seen (for example) from the output of Pelican Books, the Penguin non-fiction imprint founded in 1936 which included Wells, Haldane, Julian Huxley, Sir James Jeans, J. G. Crowther, A. N. Whitehead, and Sigmund Freud among its first authors. (Still more remarkably, the third Pelican to be published was Stapledon's science-fiction novel *Last and First Men*.) The cause of popular education was also furthered by Wells's *Outline of History*, followed by his surveys of contemporary biology, *The Science of Life* (co-authored with Julian Huxley and G. P. Wells), and of sociology and economics, *The Work, Wealth and Happiness of Mankind*. To these may be added *Mathematics for the Million* and *Science for the Citizen* (1936 and 1938 respectively) by Wells's admirer Lancelot Hogben. At a more essayistic level, the scientific outlook was propagated by J. B. S. Haldane in widely read books such as *Daedalus: or Science and the Future* (1924) and *Possible Worlds* (1927). The classic exposition of the world-view of the Scientific Enlightenment is, however, J. D. Bernal's first book, *The World, the Flesh and the Devil* (1929). Haldane's main work was to lie in genetics, while Bernal was a physicist and the author of standard books on the history and social function of science. After the mid-1930s their interest in the visionary horizons of science was obscured, though not obliterated, by commitment to the Communist cause. Both men were invited to address the British

12 Gary Werskey, *The Visible College: A Collective Biography of British Scientists and Socialists of the 1930s* (London: Free Association, 1988), p. 187.

13 C. H. Waddington, *The Scientific Attitude*, 2nd edn (West Drayton: Penguin, 1948), p. 35.

Interplanetary Society in the 1950s, and an unfinished utopian novel from the same period, found among Haldane's posthumous papers, was published as *The Man with Two Memories* (1976).

Haldane's greatest contribution to science fiction was doubtless an indirect one, of the kind that Arthur C. Clarke acknowledged in his essay 'Haldane and Space'[14]—though his friend Julian Huxley, later to become the first Director-General of UNESCO, wrote a story, 'The Tissue-Culture King' (1927), which was first published in the *Yale Review* and quickly reprinted in Gernsback's *Amazing Stories*. Haldane's sister Naomi Mitchison also includes science fiction, such as her novel *Memoirs of a Spacewoman* (1962), among her prolific fictional output.[15] *Daedalus*, the brief pamphlet which launched the 'Today and Tomorrow' series conceived by C. K. Ogden, is a wonderfully provocative statement of Haldane's scientific creed. It is partly a meditation on the place of biological invention in history and partly a work of prophetic speculation, involving a characteristic science-fictional device: an essay on the development of twentieth-century biology written by a Cambridge student 150 years hence. The principal innovation that he reports is the near-universal adoption of ectogenetic (or artificial) motherhood, leading to the separation of reproduction from sexual intercourse.

Daedalus is notable for its idiosyncratic blend of patrician classicism (Haldane was an Old Etonian) and scientific romanticism. It portrays the biologist as 'the most romantic figure on earth at the present day' (p. 77). From time to time, Haldane's vein of prophecy irresistibly turns to parody. The prototype of all genetic experiments, he explains, was the cunning wooden apparatus designed by Daedalus to enable Queen Pasiphaë to consummate her passion for a white bull, leading to the birth of the Minotaur. 'Had the housing and feeding of the Minotaur been less expensive, it is probable that Daedalus would have anticipated Mendel' (p. 47). Later on, the future undergraduate's essay on twentieth-century biology includes an airy account of an accident in 1942, when a new strain of fertiliser escaped from the laboratory and caused the Atlantic to set to a jelly.

The best of Haldane's scientific essays, such as 'The Last Judgment' and 'Possible Worlds', set out to look at existence 'from the point of

14 Arthur C. Clarke, 'Haldane and Space', in *Report on Planet Three and Other Speculations* (London: Corgi, 1973), pp. 236–43.

15 See Patrick Parrinder, 'Siblings in Space: The Science Fiction of J. B. S. Haldane and Naomi Mitchison', *Foundation* 22 (June 1981), pp. 49–56.

view of non-human minds'.[16] 'The Last Judgment' includes a
description of the end of the world as witnessed by human colonists
on Venus, while 'Possible Worlds' imagines the world of nature as it
might appear to a dog, a bee, and a barnacle, as well as one or two
more hypothetical animals. Haldane and Bernal directly influenced
such writers as Stapledon, James Blish and C. S. Lewis, as well as
Arthur C. Clarke. Bernal's The World, the Flesh and the Devil may have
had a wider importance as a source of ideas for the American pulp
magazines, since it contains concise technical descriptions of
rocketry, weightlessness, and the construction of space stations in
addition to speculations about mankind's ultimate destiny.

Bernal's 'space stations' are, in fact, celestial cities of up to 30,000
inhabitants made out of hollowed-out asteroids. Each space station
is a self-contained ecosystem, so that all waste matter has to be
recycled. It is in one of these vessels that the first group of men would
venture outside the solar system—a journey taking hundreds of
years and only to be accomplished by the remote descendants of the
original adventurers. In speculating as to who these explorers will
be, Bernal suggests that mankind may eventually divide up into two
species, the scientists and the others. The scientists would colonise
the heavens, but would continue to regard their earthbound
inferiors with a 'curious reverence': 'The world might, in fact, be
transformed into a human zoo, a zoo so intelligently managed that
its inhabitants are not aware that they are there merely for the
purposes of observation and experiment'.[17]

The combination of technical handbook to space flight and dream
of a scientific élite makes The World, the Flesh and the Devil remarkably
close to the outlook of science fiction in the 1930s and 1940s. Where
Bernal differs from Gernsback and his heirs is in his insistence on the
moral, physical and intellectual transformation of humanity which
must accompany space exploration. Ultimately his vision is of a
breaking-down of the barriers of individuality, like that which was to
be depicted in Olaf Stapledon's Star Maker:

> Finally, consciousness itself may end or vanish in a human-
> ity that has become completely etherialized, losing the
> close-knit organism, becoming masses of atoms in space

16 J. B. S. Haldane, Possible Worlds and Other Essays (London: Chatto &
Windus, 1927), p. 285.

17 J. D. Bernal, The World, the Flesh and the Devil: An Inquiry into the Future
of the Three Enemies of the Rational Soul, 2nd edn (London: Cape, 1970), p. 71.

communicating by radiation, and ultimately perhaps resolving itself entirely into light. That may be an end or a beginning, but from here it is out of sight. (p. 46)

Bernal was aware that the prospect of a dissolution of individuality, however poetic in expression, must prove abhorrent to many people. He admits the extent of the 'distaste and hatred' that have been caused by the present stage of the technological revolution (p. 55), and believes, as we have seen, that the conflict between 'humanizers' and 'mechanizers' may eventually lead to a dimorphism of the human race. This is an ingenious attempt to patch over a basic contradiction of scientific materialism—that, despite its promises, it cannot conceivably be adequate to fulfil the hopes of all human beings. This underlying contradiction may account for the failure of Haldane's and Bernal's successors as scientific popularisers to display a comparable degree of intellectual authority and visionary confidence. As early as *The Social Function of Science* (1939) Bernal was noting a general loss of enthusiasm for scientific progress.[18]

Two groups who did not share this loss of enthusiasm were, firstly, the 'hard core' of American science fiction writers, and, secondly, the ruling élite in the Soviet Union. In America Gernsback, John W. Campbell and their 'stables' of writers saw it as part of their role to convert their mainly adolescent readers to science and the scientific attitude. Of all the writers for the magazines, it was Isaac Asimov who wrote most prolifically in this cause. While Asimov's robot stories are deliberate attempts to counteract the Faustian view of technology as inherently self-destructive, his numerous books and essays on popular science often read like a vulgar-scientific parody of Haldane and Bernal. Despite his PhD in biochemistry, his outlook is that of a pragmatic, self-confident entrepreneur rather than a biologist or physicist.

In *View from a Height* (1963)—a collection of articles reprinted from the *Magazine of Fantasy and Science Fiction*—Asimov discussed the most efficient means of exploiting the planets and asteroids of the solar system. Jupiter, he suggested, should be colonised, both for its helium and because it could contain life which might turn out to be edible![19] The radioactive waste-disposal problem on earth could be

18 J. D. Bernal, *The Social Function of Science* (London: Routledge, 1939), p. 380.

19 Isaac Asimov, 'By Jove!' in *View from a Height* (London: Scientific Book Club, 1964), p. 237.

solved by creating an 'off-limits' area of space for dumping poisonous residues. Eventually, the planets should be broken up into asteroids to produce the maximum surface-area of real estate for potential settlers. The earth itself might be left intact as a museum (an echo of Bernal?) or, if the 'Progressives' outvoted the 'Traditionalists' on this issue, it too would be blown apart. The book concludes with the vision of a cosmic work-fleet advancing to accomplish this operation, all in the name of scientific progress.[20] If Asimov's science was a prop for ruthless free enterprise, Bernal and Haldane tried to combine scientific materialism with social justice by turning to Soviet Marxism. Both men became active Communist supporters in the 1930s, in response to the rise of Fascism, and both became embroiled in the post-war Lysenko controversy, which revealed the extent to which Soviet scientific research was, like all other forms of intellectual work, subject to Party control. Though committed to the idea of a classless society, the works of Bernal and Haldane show a suppressed tendency toward scientific élitism, to viewing the scientist as a member of a privileged caste. (In Haldane's case, his personal struggle with élitism was dramatically manifested in his emigration to India in the last years of his life.)

IV

Behind the barrage of early twentieth-century prophecies of space travel, eugenics and the prolongation of life lay the implication that these things were intrinsically desirable, and those who opposed them Luddite reactionaries. This was still more true of the popularisation of scientific materialism in the science-fiction magazines. The 'hard SF' of the 1930–60 period often gives the impression of mindless technology-worship. At the same time, the fetishism of technology was accompanied by its opposite, an anti-scientific fantasy literature using the settings and situations of science fiction but resorting to magic and sorcery to resolve any difficulty. This split in popular science fiction, which was to become increasingly obvious, was reflected in the controversy between J. B. S. Haldane and the novelist, scholar and Christian apologist C. S. Lewis in the 1940s.

Lewis's space trilogy, *Out of the Silent Planet* (1938), *Perelandra* (1943) and *That Hideous Strength* (1945), was intended as an attack on 'scientism'—the term he uses to denote uncritical acceptance of

20 Isaac Asimov, 'Superficially Speaking', in *View from a Height*, pp. 251–52.

scientific aims and methods as good in themselves. Lewis's brilliant imagination of alien worlds is the redeeming feature of a sequence in which plot and characterisation are, for the most part, heavily didactic. Corresponding to the three volumes of the trilogy there are three stages in his parodic unmasking of contemporary science and scientists. In *Out of the Silent Planet* the physicist Weston is a Machiavellian figure in league with big business to destroy both liberty on earth and the culture and ecology of any planet he may visit. He justifies this by his fanatical belief in the overriding glory of human destiny as foreseen by science—a belief which is simply a new form of imperialism. In *Perelandra*, Weston abandons this doctrine of 'human racism' for belief in a Wellsian 'finite God' which can be identified with the cosmic process of nature. (In keeping with Lewis's general thesis of diabolism, this change of front is the result of possession by the Devil.) *That Hideous Strength* turns back to the human world to show scientists, administrators and the popular novelist Horace Jules (H. G. Wells) as collaborators in a sinister research establishment, NICE, dedicated to a form of social control which amounts to Fascist oppression. What is remarkable about this (in some ways very silly) novel is its anticipation of some of the most popular themes of late twentieth-century fantasy fiction. Lewis's reduction of modern history to a struggle between two immemorial secret conspiracies, and his reliance on the beneficence of occult forces mediated through a small community of ordinary and apparently defenceless people in a pastoral setting, are features which could be paralleled many times over. Both the form and substance of his attack on scientism have turned out to be surprisingly far-sighted.

Haldane took Lewis's trilogy seriously enough to make it the subject of an article in the *Modern Quarterly*, the Communist Party theoretical journal, in 1946. His scornful response to Lewis's accusation of devil-worship is reflected in the title of his essay, 'Auld Hornie, F.R.S.' He has little difficulty in exposing the pseudo-scientific expedients of Lewis's plots and the hostile caricatures of individual scientific morality that the books contain. Lewis did not choose to defend himself against these charges, but an unpublished 'Reply to Professor Haldane' was included in his posthumous collection of essays, *Of Other Worlds*. Here Lewis argues rather feebly that Haldane had misunderstood his intentions, and sets out to justify the use of pseudo-scientific concepts in science fiction so long as they do not contravene the 'folk science' necessary to secure the ordinary reader's suspension of disbelief. (Here it may be noted that his practice—such as, for example, describing the 'canals' on Mars—has the almost unanimous endorsement of science-fiction writers.) For his major point, however, the reader is referred back to *The Abolition of Man* (1943), a book in which Lewis set out the philosophical position underlying the trilogy. The commitment to the subjugation of nature fundamental to modern science, he argues, is necessarily a commitment to the subjugation of 'man' as well. In answer to the technologists' programme of human 'abolition' Lewis dreams wistfully of a 'regenerate science' which resembles the most extreme yearnings of present-day ecologists. Such a science, he writes, 'would not do even to minerals and vegetables what modern science threatens to do to man himself'.[21] Lewis's ideal is not even 'pastoral'—since it threatens the very existence of agriculture—but, unfortunately, absurd; it would mean the elimination alike of nature and of human history.

Lewis's appeal to literary and religious values against those of science is in some ways reminiscent of a later and much better publicised British *cause célèbre*, the quarrel between C. P. Snow and the literary critic F. R. Leavis in the early 1960s. While the debate that it provoked has little relevance to science fiction, Snow's lecture *The Two Cultures and the Scientific Revolution* (1959) was a memorable statement of scientific materialism by a novelist who was very much a disciple of men like Wells and Haldane. However, in terms of the history traced in this chapter, one of the most striking features of Snow's lecture is its belatedness. Snow argues that Western intellectual life is polarised between literary and scientific 'cultures', but it was only in a later essay. 'The Two Cultures: A Second Look' (1963), that he noted the imminent emergence of a 'third culture' of social scientists taking as their province the human effects of the scientific revolution. But by that time science fiction had already made its substantial shift from prophetic endorsement to parody of the world-view of the Scientific Enlightenment.

V

At the beginning of his history of the atomic scientists, *Brighter Than a Thousand Suns* (1956), Robert Jungk records a conversation with a central European scientist at Los Alamos in 1949. 'What an extra-

---

21 C. S. Lewis, *The Abolition of Man, or Reflections on Education with Special Reference to the Teaching of English in the Upper Forms of Schools* (London: Oxford University Press, 1943), p. 39.

ordinary and incomprehensible thing!' the scientist said. 'My whole youth was absolutely devoted to truth, freedom, and peace; yet fate has seen fit to deposit me here where my freedom of movement is limited; the truth that I am trying to discover is locked behind massive gates; and the ultimate aim of my work has to be the construction of the most hideous weapons of war'.[22] The destructive potential of nuclear energy had been evident since the beginning of the twentieth century, and it epitomises, in a terrible symbol, the darker side of the Scientific Enlightenment. Frederick Soddy, Rutherford's collaborator and the author of *The Interpretation of Radium* (1908), was one of those who heralded the dawn of an 'entirely new civilisation' made possible by the latest scientific discoveries: 'This is the message of hope and inspiration to the race which radium has contributed to the great problems of existence', he wrote.[23] Disillusionment spread very swiftly after the atomic bombs were dropped on Hiroshima and Nagasaki in 1945. Not only did scientists in the early Cold War years respond to the growth of the military-industrial complex with a campaign to enlighten the public about the dangers of nuclear energy, but so many 'atomic doom' stories appeared in the science fiction magazines that by 1948 John W. Campbell felt obliged to tell his writers that such stories were no longer wanted.[24] In the 1960s, after the vogue for 'realistic' novels and films of nuclear catastrophe such as Nevil Shute's *On the Beach*, the generation of science fiction writers loosely known as the New Wave began to exploit post-nuclear nightmares as a way of questioning the scientific enterprise as a whole. The most influential writer in this mode was J. G. Ballard.

Ballard is the poet of the Scientific Enlightenment in decline. While he has run through the gamut of science-fictional prophecies, from tomorrow's disasters to the ultimate achievement of union with the cosmos ('The Waiting Ground', 1967), he has often argued that our 'myths of the near future' are merely extrapolative, a projection of essentially contemporary wishes and needs. Several of his stories amount to a composite history of the failure of the Space Age. 'The Cage of Sand' (1963) shows a group of fugitives infected with a dangerous Martian virus lurking in an abandoned and

22 Robert Jungk, *Brighter Than a Thousand Suns* (Harmondsworth: Penguin, 1960), p. 11.

23 Frederick Soddy, *The Interpretation of Radium*, pp. 239, 252.

24 Paul A. Carter, *The Creation of Tomorrow*, pp. 250–51.

quarantined Cape Canaveral. 'Thirteen for Centaurus' describes an earthbound spaceship whose crew have been tricked into believing they are on a hundred-year voyage to Alpha Centauri. ' "What began as a grand adventure in the spirit of Columbus" ', one of the characters moralises, ' "has become a grisly joke" '.[25] The tone of hard-boiled disillusion with science is the stock-in-trade of these stories.

Ballard's parodic inversion of the scientific outlook may be seen by glancing at one of his favourite metaphors, the 'terminal beach'. As an apocalyptic symbol this presumably derives from *The Time Machine*, where in the 'Further Vision' the beach is the last stronghold of life as it regresses back to the sea. Ballard's beaches belong to the immediate future. Typical of them are the half-submerged landscape of London in *The Drowned World* (1962), the beach crowded with sunbathers waiting for a satellite launching in 'The Reptile Enclosure' (1964) and the post-nuclear wasteland of Eniwetok Island in 'The Terminal Beach' (1964). Biological regression is hinted at in all these stories. The fauna and flora of the Triassic Age are re-created in *The Drowned World*. In 'The Reptile Enclosure', infra-red radiation from the satellite sets off 'innate releasing mechanisms' inherited from our Cro-Magnon ancestors which drive the sunbathing crowds like lemmings into the sea. Eniwetok is a source of pilgrimage for the 'possessed'—like Ballard's character Traven—who find it an 'ontological Garden of Eden'.[26] In the Cape Canaveral stories, the beaches of Florida are the appropriate setting for humanity's forlorn attempt to establish a beachhead in space. But although the theory of evolution is used as an adjunct to Ballard's visions of environmental disaster, it is clear that the main 'scientific' background for these stories is not biology, as it was for Wells, but Jungian psychology. The sea towards which life regresses stands for the womb, just as outer space stands in Ballard's work for inner space. He is, in a sense, correct in implying that the concern with the very long-term future found in Wells and his successors is a sublimation of present-day anxieties. However, the cumulative effect of Ballard's fictions is reductive in the extreme. The more he extends his range to new areas of social experience, whether those of

25 J. G. Ballard, 'Thirteen for Centaurus', in *The Best Short Stories of J. G. Ballard* (New York: Holt, Rinehart & Winston, 1978), p. 159.
26 J. G. Ballard, 'The Terminal Beach', in *The Best Short Stories of J. G. Ballard*, p. 263.

the car crash, the high-rise apartment block or the urban homeless imprisoned on their 'concrete islands', the more he eliminates the sense of scientific possibility. His heroes are trapped spectators sharing some of their creator's relish for the aesthetics of decay and destruction.

Like his predecessors, Ballard is a master of the mode of literary prophecy. The author's biography attached to the Penguin editions of his books in the 1960s proclaims his view that science fiction is 'the apocalyptic literature of the twentieth century, the authentic language of Auschwitz, Eniwetok and Aldermaston'. No other writer of his time has explored so many varieties of apocalypse, and his fascination with the end of the grand narrative of scientific modernity is only equalled by his ability to extract from it a long series of grisly jokes. Ballard's early career was that of a wartime internee, a medical student, an advertising copywriter and an RAF pilot—but not a practising scientist. His British contemporary Brian Aldiss worked as a bookseller and literary editor before turning to science fiction. In the United States too, the generation of writers and editors formed by the Scientific Enlightenment—Asimov, Blish, Campbell, Heinlein, Jack Williamson and others—was succeeded by a generation in which the leading figures had received little or no formal scientific education. This is true, for example, of Samuel Delany, Philip K. Dick, Harlan Ellison, Ursula K. Le Guin (though Le Guin is the daughter of two famous anthropologists), and Robert Silverberg. Today the aspiring science-fiction writer is more likely to be an English teacher than a research student in physics. Harlan Ellison (b.1934) may be the first such writer to have terminated his education by getting himself kicked out, not from a science lab, but from a creative writing class. Would it be too simple to say (though Aldiss for one has said it)[27] that these writers and their successors are less influenced by the vision of science than by the literary precedents of earlier science fiction?[28]

VI

Hostile parody of the Scientific Enlightenment, as in Lewis's novels or in the reference to a 'Huxdane-Halley bomb (for the dissemi-

27 Brian Aldiss, *The Shape of Further Things*, p. 127.

28 However, the influence of popular nineteenth-century scientific romances on Wells should not be underestimated.

nation of leprosy germs)' in Evelyn Waugh's *Vile Bodies* (1930),[29] was always to be expected. However, this chapter will end by considering how in one representative aspect the scientific-materialist outlook lends itself to parody even among those committed to scientific perspectives. A contemporary physicist, Steven Weinberg, has written of the 'expanding universe' that 'the more [it] seems comprehensible, the more it also seems pointless'.[30] That view, if generally accepted, would surely lead to the diversion of new students into other fields, academic redundancies, and the drying-up of research grants. Science fiction (whether optimistic or pessimistic) has traditionally cooperated with the scientific institution by making its cosmological and futurological perspectives seem more meaningful to the individual reader than, perhaps, they really were. Hence a cosmos populated by aliens and robots who talk and behave like recognisable beings, an intergalactic politics which closely resembles terrestrial politics, and the various kinds of 'space-drive' or 'hyperdrive' to cross the apparently insuperable barrier of the speed of light. For much of the past half-century it seemed increasingly difficult to sustain the genre's 'domestication' of the universe without resorting either to stale conventions or to a blatant use of pseudo-science.

Since space and time on their own appear to be infinitely extensible, it may appear paradoxical that the idea of a space-time system, 'world-enveloping' in Thomas Carlyle's phrase, can come to be represented as a kind of prison. However, nineteenth-century Positivism had already made of the space-time continuum a kind of diagram or grid. This idea, which originates with Pierre Laplace,[31] implies that the future must eventually be as knowable as the past. As a science student in the 1880s, Wells imagined a 'Universal Diagram' from which, as he recalled in his *Autobiography*, 'all phenomena would be derived by a process of deduction' (I, p. 214). Poe's *Eureka*, with its description of the universe alternately expanding and contracting for evermore like the air in a pair of bellows, is a *reductio ad absurdum* of the eschatology of a world-picture like this.

From most points of view, the idea of a 'Universe Rigid', as Wells

29 Evelyn Waugh, *Vile Bodies* (Harmondsworth: Penguin, 1938), p. 221.

30 Steven Weinberg, *The First Three Minutes: A Modern View of the Origin of the Universe* (London: Deutsch, 1977), p. 154.

31 See Stephen Kern, *The Culture of Time and Space 1880–1918* (Cambridge, Mass.: Harvard University Press, 1983), pp. 100–01.

called it, is indeed an absurdity. Wells himself was the first to disown or at least qualify it. But it can be argued that the spectre of the Universal Diagram still haunts modern science fiction, underscoring its most prophetic effects with an element of parody. The effect of most time-travel and time-loop stories, for example, is to make the universe a smaller, more predictable and more repetitive place. Fables of universal entropy deliberately set out to produce an atmosphere of near-claustrophobic enclosure. Yet even where the reverse effect seems to be intended, in space operas full of teleportation, instantaneous communication, space-warp, time-jumping and so on, the impression of frenetic movement does little to dispel an ultimate sense of enclosure. In his 1981 novel *Valis*, Philip K. Dick suggests that everyone who has ever lived is unknowingly trapped within the 'Black Iron Prison' of a rigid space-time universe. Only a few favoured people (in Dick's eccentric world, neo-Christian mystics) can escape from this prison.[32] The fact of universal enclosure is insisted upon in such openly parodic and comic science fiction as Kurt Vonnegut's *The Sirens of Titan* (1963) and in Douglas Adams's popular space operas *The Hitch-Hiker's Guide to the Galaxy* (1978) and *The Restaurant at the End of the Universe* (1980). More recently, cyberpunk science fiction reduces cosmological space-time to the virtual reality of the electronic interface.

In *Studies in Human Time*, Georges Poulet finds in Bergson the prototype of a twentieth-century understanding of time which abolishes the determinism of a 'Universe Rigid'. Theories of gratuitous action and existential choice stress 'the feeling that any moment can be expressed as a new moment, and that time can always be freely created from the present moment forward'.[33] Similarly, in Relativity theory the measurement of time and space depends entirely on the position of the observer. Wells seems to have anticipated that in the strange chapter of *The First Men in the Moon* called 'Mr Bedford in Infinite Space', where the narrator finds himself released, so far as he can tell, from normal duration and the confines of his bodily identity. Travelling back to earth on his own he has the idea that 'really I was something quite outside not only the world, but all worlds, and out of space and time, and that this poor Bedford was just a peephole through which I looked at life' (Ch. 20).

32 Philip K. Dick, *Valis* (New York: Bantam, 1981), pp. 40–41.
33 Georges Poulet, *Studies in Human Time*, trans. Elliott Coleman (Baltimore and London: Johns Hopkins, 1956), p. 35.

Yet he returns from infinite space to earth, splashing down off the Kent coast near a village with the marvellously appropriate name of Littlestone-on-Sea. Looking back he tends to think that, like the traditional 'lunatic', once outside the earth's gravitational pull his mental balance was disturbed.

This 'cloudy megalomania' as Bedford calls it, a sort of Gnostic intimation of universal consciousness, suggests part of the inner motivation of our fascination with space travel. Similar feelings are present in other Scientific Enlightenment novelists and thinkers, notably Bernal, Clarke and Stapledon. Within the space-time system disappointment and disillusionment are almost inevitable, however, and writers must resort to conscious myth-making to deny this. In *Starman Jones* (1953) Robert Heinlein's juvenile hero explains the existence of cosmic 'anomalies' which make faster-than-light travel possible: 'If it weren't for the anomalies, there never would have been any way for us to reach the stars; the distances are too great. But looking back, it is obvious that all that emptiness couldn't be real —there *had* to be the anomalies. That's what my uncle used to say'.[34] Referring to his uncle as the source of authority, Starman Jones is the quintessential second-generation Scientific Enlightenment figure: the unconscious parodist in the footsteps of the prophet. At the same time, there is a long tradition of important discoveries made not by the sorcerer himself but, perhaps inadvertently, by his nephew or apprentice. If prophecy turns to parody, parody can also turn into prophecy.

Today the most exciting developments in cosmology result from the reconvergence of mathematics and physics. The search for a unifying physical theory, it has been realised, is vastly simplified by moving from four-dimensional space-time to higher-dimensional space. The branch of multi-dimensional geometry known as 'string theory' has led to the positing of a ten-dimensional universe split into two parts, one of which is the familiar universe and the other its 'dwarf twin', a 'six-dimensional ball that is too small to be observed'.[35] As the one expands, the other contracts, and vice versa. Moreover, there is much discussion of so-called 'wormholes' in space-time, connecting different universes or different areas of the same universe together. Experimental verification of such theories is

34 Robert A. Heinlein, *Starman Jones* (New York: Ballantine, 1975), p. 80.

35 Michio Kaku, *Hyperspace*, p. 27.

currently impossible, and in some respects they sound like a parody of the science-fictional universe, and even of Mr Bedford's experiences in infinite space. Steven Weinberg, who wrote in 1977 of the apparent pointlessness of the universe, commented recently that theoretical physics seemed to be becoming more and more like science fiction.[36] In 1988 the scientific journal *Physics Review Letters* published what has been described as 'the first serious proposal for a time machine'.[37] It is conceivable that the ferment of cosmological thinking at the end of the twentieth century could give birth to a new science fiction, not merely to further elaborations on the existing pattern. But it still awaits its prophet; and in trying to imagine a future science fiction we are for the time being grasping at shadows.

36 Ibid., p. 9.
37 Ibid., p. 245.

Select Bibliography

Note on Bibliographical Sources

The forthcoming bibliography by David C. Smith will give a complete listing of Wells's published writings (more than 1200 items) for the first time. The most up-to-date bibliographies currently available are: *H. G. Wells: A Comprehensive Bibliography*, 4th edn (London: The H. G. Wells Society, 1986); *Herbert George Wells: An Annotated Bibliography of His Works*, ed. J. R. Hammond (New York & London: Garland, 1977); and *H. G. Wells: A Reference Guide* by William J. Scheick and J. Randolph Cox (Boston: Hall, 1988). See also the regular listings of new items on Wells in the *Wellsian*.

(i) Chronology of H. G. Wells's Principal Writings

The name of the publisher is given in brackets. Place of publication is London unless otherwise stated.

1893   *A Textbook of Biology* (Clive), *Honours Physiography* (with R. A. Gregory) (Hughes)

1895   *Select Conversations with an Uncle* (Lane), *The Time Machine* (Heinemann), *The Wonderful Visit* (Dent), *The Stolen Bacillus and Other Incidents* (Methuen)

1896   *The Island of Doctor Moreau* (Heinemann), *The Wheels of Chance* (Dent)

1897   *The Plattner Story and Others* (Methuen), *The Invisible Man* (Pearson), *Certain Personal Matters* (Lawrence & Bullen)

1898   *The War of the Worlds* (Heinemann)

1899   *When the Sleeper Wakes* (Harper), *Tales of Space and Time* (Harper)

1900   *Love and Mr Lewisham* (Harper)

1901   *The First Men in the Moon* (Newnes), *Anticipations* (Chapman & Hall)

1902   *The Discovery of the Future* (Unwin), *The Sea Lady* (Methuen)

1903   *Mankind in the Making* (Chapman & Hall), *Twelve Stories and a Dream* (Macmillan)

1904   *The Food of the Gods* (Macmillan)

1905   *A Modern Utopia* (Chapman & Hall), *Kipps* (Macmillan)

1906   *In the Days of the Comet* (Macmillan), *The Future in America* (Chapman & Hall)

1908   *New Worlds for Old* (Constable), *The War in the Air* (Bell), *First and Last Things* (Constable)

1909   *Tono-Bungay* (Macmillan), *Ann Veronica* (Unwin)

1910   *The History of Mr Polly* (Nelson)

1911   *The New Machiavelli* (Lane), *The Country of the Blind and Other Stories* (Nelson)

1912   *The Great State* (with 12 other authors) (Harper), *Marriage* (Macmillan)

1913   *The Passionate Friends* (Macmillan)

1914   *An Englishman Looks at the World* (Cassell), *The World Set Free* (Macmillan), *The Wife of Sir Isaac Harman* (Macmillan), *The War that Will End War* (Palmer)

1915   *Boon* (Unwin), *Bealby* (Methuen), *The Research Magnificent* (Macmillan)

1916   *What Is Coming* (Cassell), *Mr Britling Sees It Through* (Cassell)

1917   *War and the Future* (Cassell), *God the Invisible King* (Cassell), *The Soul of a Bishop* (Cassell)

1918   *In the Fourth Year* (Chatto & Windus), *Joan and Peter* (Cassell)

1919   *The Undying Fire* (Cassell)

1920   *The Outline of History* (Newnes), *Russia in the Shadows* (Hodder & Stoughton)

1921   *The Salvaging of Civilisation* (Cassell)

1922   *Washington and the Hope of Peace* (Collins), *The Secret Places of the Heart* (Cassell), *A Short History of the World* (Cassell)

1923   *Men Like Gods* (Cassell)

1924   *The Story of a Great Schoolmaster* (Chatto & Windus), *The Dream* (Cape), *A Year of Prophesying* (Unwin)

1924–27   *The Atlantic Edition of the Works of H. G. Wells* (Unwin)

1925   *Christina Alberta's Father* (Cape)

1926   *The World of William Clissold* (Benn)

1927   *Meanwhile* (Benn), *The Complete Short Stories of H. G. Wells* (Benn)

1928   *The Way the World Is Going* (Benn), *The Open Conspiracy* (Gollancz), *Mr Blettsworthy on Rampole Island* (Benn)
1929   *The King Who Was a King* (Benn)
1930   *The Autocracy of Mr Parham* (Heinemann), *The Science of Life* (with Julian Huxley and G. P. Wells) (Amalgamated Press)
1931   *What Are We To Do With Our Lives?* (Heinemann), *The Work, Wealth and Happiness of Mankind* (New York: Doubleday, Doran)
1932   *After Democracy* (Watts), *The Bulpington of Blup* (Hutchinson)
1933   *The Shape of Things to Come* (Hutchinson)
1934   *Experiment in Autobiography* (Gollancz), *Stalin-Wells Talk* (New Statesman)
1935   *The New America: The New World* (Cresset Press), *Things to Come* (Cresset Press)
1936   *The Anatomy of Frustration* (Cresset Press), *The Croquet Player* (Chatto & Windus)
1937   *Star Begotten* (Chatto & Windus), *Brynhild* (Methuen), *The Camford Visitation* (Methuen)
1938   *The Brothers* (Chatto & Windus), *World Brain* (Methuen), *Apropos of Dolores* (Cape)
1939   *The Holy Terror* (Joseph), *Travels of a Republican Radical in Search of Hot Water* (Penguin), *The Fate of Homo Sapiens* (Secker & Warburg), *The New World Order* (Secker & Warburg)
1940   *The Rights of Man* (Penguin), *Babes in the Darkling Wood* (Secker & Warburg), *The Common Sense of War and Peace* (Penguin), *All Aboard for Ararat* (Secker & Warburg)
1941   *Guide to the New World* (Gollancz), *You Can't Be Too Careful* (Secker & Warburg)
1942   *The Outlook for Homo Sapiens* (Secker & Warburg), *Science and the World-Mind* (New Europe), *Phoenix* (Secker & Warburg), *The Conquest of Time* (Watts)
1943   *Crux Ansata* (Penguin)
1944   *'42 to '44* (Secker & Warburg)
1945   *The Happy Turning* (Heinemann), *Mind at the End of Its Tether* (Heinemann)

(ii) Posthumous works

1964   *Journalism and Prophecy 1893–1946*, ed. W. Warren Wagar (Boston: Houghton Mifflin)

1969   *The Wealth of Mr Waddy*, ed. Harris Wilson (Carbondale and Edwardsville: Southern Illinois University Press)

1975   *Early Writings in Science and Science Fiction*, ed. Robert M. Philmus and David Y. Hughes (Berkeley, Los Angeles and London: University of California Press)

1980   *H. G. Wells's Literary Criticism*, ed. Patrick Parrinder and Robert M. Philmus (Brighton: Harvester Press, and Totowa, N.J.: Barnes & Noble)

1984   *H. G. Wells in Love*, ed. G. P. Wells (Faber & Faber), *The Man with a Nose and Other Uncollected Short Stories*, ed. J. R. Hammond (Athlone Press)

(iii) Scholarly editions of Wells's science fiction

A Critical Edition of 'The War of the Worlds': H. G. Wells's *Scientific Romance* with Introduction and Notes by David Y. Hughes and Harry M. Geduld. (Bloomington and Indianapolis: Indiana University Press, 1993)

The Definitive 'Time Machine': A Critical Edition of H. G. Wells's Scientific Romance with Introduction and Notes by Harry M. Geduld. (Bloomington and Indianapolis: Indiana University Press, 1987).

The First Men in the Moon edited with an Introduction by David Lake (The World's Classics). (New York: Oxford University Press, 1995)

The Island of Doctor Moreau: A Variorum Text edited by Robert M. Philmus. (Athens, Ga. and London: University of Georgia Press, 1993)

The War of the Worlds edited by David Y. Hughes with an Introduction by Brian W. Aldiss (The World's Classics). (New York: Oxford University Press, 1995)

(iv) Uncollected writings by H. G. Wells cited in the text

This list excludes writings collected in works listed in sections (ii) and (iii) above.

'George Gissing: An Impression' (*Monthly Review*, August 1904), reprinted in Royal A. Gettmann, ed., *George Gissing and H. G. Wells:*

Their Friendship and Correspondence (London: Hart–Davis, 1961), pp. 260–77.

'Mr Wells Explains Himself', *T.P.'s Magazine* (December 1911).

'Socrates', *Science Schools Journal* I:1 (December 1886), pp. 18–21.

'A Tale of the Twentieth Century: For Advanced Thinkers', *Science Schools Journal* I:6 (May 1887) pp. 187–91, reprinted in Bernard Bergonzi, *The Early H. G. Wells: A Study of the Scientific Romances* (Manchester: Manchester University Press, 1961), pp. 181–86.

'Utopias' (1939), *Science-Fiction Studies* 27 (July 1982), pp. 117–21.

(v) Secondary works: H. G. Wells

Aldiss, Brian W. 'Wells and the Leopard Lady', in Patrick Parrinder and Christopher Rolfe, eds., *H. G. Wells Under Revision*, pp. 27–39; also in Brian W. Aldiss, *The Detached Retina: Aspects of SF and Fantasy* (Liverpool: Liverpool University Press, 1995), pp. 116–27.

Batchelor, John. *H. G. Wells* (Cambridge: Cambridge University Press, 1985).

Bellamy, William. *The Novels of Wells, Bennett and Galsworthy 1890–1910* (London: Routledge & Kegan Paul, 1971).

Bergonzi, Bernard. *The Early H. G. Wells: A Study of the Scientific Romances* (Manchester: Manchester University Press, 1961).

Bergonzi, Bernard. '*The Time Machine*: An Ironic Myth', in Bernard Bergonzi, ed., *H. G. Wells: A Collection of Critical Essays*, pp. 39–55.

Bergonzi, Bernard (ed.). *H. G. Wells: A Collection of Critical Essays* (Englewood Cliffs, N.J.: Prentice-Hall, 1976).

Brooks, Van Wyck. *The World of H. G. Wells* (London: Unwin, 1915).

Brown, Richard. 'On Triviality in the Naive Comic Fictions of H. G. Wells', *Cahiers Victoriens et Edouardiens* 30 (October 1989), pp. 55–66.

Crossley, Robert. 'In the Palace of Green Porcelain: Artifacts from the Museums of Science Fiction', in Tom Shippey, ed., *Fictional Space: Essays on Contemporary Science Fiction* (Oxford: Blackwell and Atlantic Highlands, N.J.: Humanities Press, 1991), pp. 76–103.

Draper, Michael. *H. G. Wells* (Basingstoke: Macmillan, 1987).

Draper, Michael. 'The Martians in Ecuador', *Wellsian* ns5 (Summer 1982), pp. 35–36.

Eliot, T. S. 'Wells as Journalist', in Patrick Parrinder, ed., *H. G. Wells: The Critical Heritage*, pp. 319–22.

Gettmann, Royal A., ed. *George Gissing and H. G. Wells: Their Friendship and Correspondence* (London: Hart-Davis, 1961).

Hammond, J. R. *An H. G. Wells Companion* (London and Basingstoke: Macmillan, 1979).

Hammond, J. R. *H. G. Wells and the Modern Novel* (Basingstoke: Macmillan, 1988).

Haynes, Roslynn D. *H. G. Wells: Discoverer of the Future: The Influence of Science on his Thought* (London and Basingstoke: Macmillan, 1980).

Hillegas, Mark R. *The Future as Nightmare: H. G. Wells and the Anti-Utopians* (New York: Oxford University Press, 1967).

Hughes, David Y. 'The Mood of *A Modern Utopia*', *Extrapolation* 19 (December 1977), pp. 59–67.

Huntington, John. *The Logic of Fantasy: H. G. Wells and Science Fiction* (New York: Columbia University Press, 1982).

Kemp, Peter. *H. G. Wells and the Culminating Ape: Biological Themes and Imaginative Obsessions* (London and Basingstoke: Macmillan, 1982).

Keun, Odette. 'H. G. Wells—The Player', *Time and Tide* (13–27 October 1934), pp. 1249–51, 1307–09, 1346–48.

Lodge, David. '*Tono-Bungay* and the Condition of England', in *Language of Fiction* (London: Routledge & Kegan Paul, 1966), pp. 214–42.

Loing, Bernard. *H. G. Wells à l'oeuvre: Les débuts d'un écrivain (1894–1900)* (Paris: Didier, 1984).

Mackenzie, Norman and Jeanne. *The Time Traveller: The Life of H. G. Wells* (London: Weidenfeld & Nicolson, 1973).

McConnell, Frank. *The Science Fiction of H. G. Wells* (New York: Oxford University Press, 1981).

Orwell, George. 'Wells, Hitler and the World State' in *Collected Essays, Journalism and Letters*, ed. Sonia Orwell and Ian Angus (London: Secker & Warburg, 1968), II, pp. 139–45.

Parrinder, Patrick. 'From Mary Shelley to *The War of the Worlds*: The Thames Valley Catastrophe', in David Seed, ed., *Anticipations: Essays on Early Science Fiction and its Precursors* (Liverpool: Liverpool University Press, 1995), pp. 58–74.

Parrinder, Patrick. *H. G. Wells* (Edinburgh: Oliver & Boyd, 1970).

Parrinder, Patrick. 'The Roman Spring of George Gissing and H. G. Wells', *Gissing Newsletter* XXI:3 (July 1985), pp. 1–12.

Parrinder, Patrick (ed.). *H. G. Wells: The Critical Heritage* (London and Boston: Routledge & Kegan Paul, 1972).

Parrinder, Patrick, and Rolfe, Christopher (eds.). *H. G. Wells Under Revision: Proceedings of the International H. G. Wells Symposium,*

London, July 1986 (Selinsgrove: Susquehanna University Press, and London and Toronto: Associated University Presses, 1990).

Philmus, Robert M. *Into the Unknown: The Evolution of Science Fiction from Francis Godwin to H. G. Wells* (Berkeley and Los Angeles: University of California Press, 1970).

Philmus, Robert M. 'The Logic of Prophecy in *The Time Machine*', in Bernard Bergonzi, ed., *H. G. Wells: A Collection of Critical Essays*, pp. 56–68.

Pritchett, V. S. 'The Scientific Romances', in Bernard Bergonzi, ed., *H. G. Wells: A Collection of Critical Essays*, pp. 32–38.

Reed, John R. *The Natural History of H. G. Wells* (Athens, Ohio: Ohio University Press, 1982).

Seed, David. 'Doctor Moreau and his Beast People', *Udolpho* 17 (June 1994), pp. 8–12.

Smith, David C. *H. G. Wells: Desperately Mortal: A Biography* (New Haven and London: Yale University Press, 1986).

Stover, Leon. 'Applied Natural History: Wells vs. Huxley', in Patrick Parrinder and Christopher Rolfe, eds., *H. G. Wells Under Revision*, pp. 125–33.

Stover, Leon. *The Prophetic Soul: A Reading of H. G. Wells's ''Things to Come* (Jefferson, N.C. and London: McFarland, 1987).

Stover, Leon. 'Spade House Dialectic: Theme and Theory in ''Things to Come'' ', *Wellsian* ns5 (1982), pp. 23–32.

Suvin, Darko, and Philmus, Robert M. (eds.). *H. G. Wells and Modern Science Fiction* (Lewisburg: Bucknell University Press, and London: Associated University Presses, 1977).

Wagar, W. Warren. *H. G. Wells and the World State* (Freeport, N.Y.: Books for Libraries Press, 1971).

West, Anthony. *H. G. Wells: Aspects of a Life* (London: Hutchinson, 1984).

West, Geoffrey. *H. G. Wells: A Sketch for a Portrait* (London: Howe, 1930).

Wilson, Harris (ed.). *Arnold Bennett and H. G. Wells: A Record of a Personal and a Literary Friendship* (London: Hart-Davis, 1960).

Zamyatin, Yevgeny. *Herbert Wells* (1922), trans. Lesley Milne, in Patrick Parrinder, ed., *H. G. Wells: The Critical Heritage*, pp. 258–74.

Zangwill, Israel. 'Without Prejudice', in Patrick Parrinder, ed., *H. G. Wells: The Critical Heritage*, pp. 40–42.

(vi) Secondary works: Science fiction and general

Aldiss, Brian. *The Shape of Further Things: Speculation on Change* (London: Corgi, 1974).

Alkon, Paul K. *Origins of Futuristic Fiction* (Athens, Ga. and London: University of Georgia Press, 1988).

Asfour, Mohammad. 'Literary Prophecy', *Abhath Al-Yarmouk: Literature and Linguistics Series* 4:1 (1986), pp. 7–18.

Asimov, Isaac. *View from a Height* (London: Scientific Book Club, 1964).

Bakhtin, M. M. *The Dialogic Imagination: Four Essays*, ed. Michael Holquist (Austin: University of Texas Press, 1981).

Bernal, J. D. *The Social Function of Science* (London: Routledge, 1939).

Bernal, J. D. *The World, the Flesh and the Devil: An Inquiry into the Future of the Three Enemies of the Rational Soul*, 2nd edn. (London: Cape, 1970).

Carlyle, Thomas. *Critical and Miscellaneous Essays* (London: Chapman & Hall, n.d.).

Carlyle, Thomas. *Past and Present* (London: Chapman & Hall, 1863).

Carlyle, Thomas. *Sartor Resartus and On Heroes* (London: Dent, 1908).

Carter, Paul A. *The Creation of Tomorrow* (New York: Columbia University Press, 1977).

Cicero, Marcus Tullius. *Brutus, On the Nature of the Gods, On Divination, On Duties*, trans. Hubert M. Poteat (Chicago: University of Chicago Press, 1950).

Clarke, Arthur C. 'The Challenge of the Spaceship', *Journal of the British Interplanetary Society* VI:3 (December 1946), pp. 66–78.

Clarke, Arthur C. *Profiles of the Future: An Enquiry into the Limits of the Possible* (London: Gollancz, 1962).

Clarke, Arthur C. *Report on Planet Three and Other Speculations* (London: Corgi, 1973).

Colls, Robert, and Dodd, Philip (eds.). *Englishness: Politics and Culture 1880–1920* (London: Croom Helm, 1986).

Darwin, Charles. *Autobiography* (London: Watts, 1929).

Darwin, Charles. *The Origin of Species by Means of Natural Selection*, 6th edn (London: Murray, 1910).

Drabkina, E. 'Memories of Lenin', *Izvestiia* (22 December 1961).

Eliot, T. S. *The Sacred Wood: Essays on Poetry and Criticism* (London: Methuen, 1960).

Flacelière, Robert. *Greek Oracles*, trans. Douglas Garman (London: Elek, 1965).

A General Guide to the British Museum (Natural History), Cromwell Road, London S.W. (London: British Museum Trustees, 1886).

George, Henry. *Progress and Poverty* (London: Dent, 1911).

Gibbon, Edward. *The Decline and Fall of the Roman Empire*, ed. Dero T. Saunders (London: Penguin, 1981).

Gibbon, Edward. *The History of the Decline and Fall of the Roman Empire*, ed. J. B. Bury (London: Methuen, 1898).

Goodwin, Barbara, and Taylor, Keith. *The Politics of Utopia: A Study in Theory and Practice* (London: Hutchinson, 1982).

Graves, Robert. *The Greek Myths* (Harmondsworth: Penguin, 1955).

Hacking, Ian. *Representing and Intervening: Introductory Topics in the Philosophy of Natural Science* (Cambridge: Cambridge University Press, 1983).

Haldane, J. B. S. 'Auld Hornie, F.R.S.', *Modern Quarterly* nsI:4 (Autumn 1946), pp. 32–40.

Haldane, J. B. S. *Daedalus: or Science and the Future* (London: Kegan Paul, 1924).

Haldane, J. B. S. *Possible Worlds and Other Essays* (London: Chatto & Windus, 1927).

Howard, Ebenezer. *Garden Cities of To-morrow*, ed. F. J. Osborn (London: Faber & Faber, 1965).

Hoyle, Fred. *Of Men and Galaxies* (London: Heinemann, 1965).

Hutcheon, Linda. *A Theory of Parody: The Teachings of Twentieth-Century Art Forms* (New York and London: Methuen, 1985).

Huxley, T. H. *Evidence as to Man's Place in Nature* (London: Williams & Norgate, 1863).

Huxley, T. H. *Evolution and Ethics and Other Essays* (London: Macmillan, 1895).

Huxley, T. H. *Methods and Results: Essays* (London: Macmillan, 1904).

James, Henry. *Selected Literary Criticism*, ed. Morris Shapira (London: Heinemann, 1963).

Jameson, Fredric. 'Progress Versus Utopia: or, Can We Imagine the Future?', *Science-Fiction Studies* 27 (July 1982), pp. 147–58.

Jungk, Robert. *Brighter than a Thousand Suns* (Harmondsworth: Penguin, 1960).

Kaku, Michio. *Hyperspace: A Scientific Odyssey Through Parallel Universes, Time Warps, and The Tenth Dimension* (New York and Oxford: Oxford University Press, 1994).

Kern, Stephen. *The Culture of Time and Space 1880–1918* (Cambridge, Mass.: Harvard University Press, 1983).

Lewis, C. S. *The Abolition of Man, or Reflections on Education with Special*

Reference to the Teaching of English in the Upper Forms of Schools (London: Oxford University Press, 1943).

Lewis, C. S. *Of Other Worlds: Essays and Stories*, ed. Walter Hooper (London: Bles, 1966).

Martin, Andrew. *The Mask of the Prophet: The Extraordinary Fictions of Jules Verne* (Oxford: Clarendon Press, 1990).

Miller, J. Hillis. *The Form of Victorian Fiction* (Notre Dame and London: University of Notre Dame Press, 1968).

Morris, William. 'Looking Backward', *Commonweal* 59 (June 22, 1889), p. 194.

Mullen, Richard D. 'Blish, van Vogt, and the Uses of Spengler', *Riverside Quarterly* III:3 (August 1968), pp. 172–80.

Nozick, Robert. *Anarchy, State and Utopia* (Oxford: Oxford University Press, 1974).

Orwell, George. *Collected Essays, Journalism and Letters*, ed. Sonia Orwell and Ian Angus (London: Secker & Warburg, 1968).

Parke, H. W. *Greek Oracles* (London: Hutchinson, 1967).

Parrinder, Patrick. *Science Fiction: Its Criticism and Teaching* (London and New York: Methuen, 1980).

Parrinder, Patrick (ed.). *Science Fiction: A Critical Guide* (London and New York: Longman, 1979).

Poulet, Georges. *Studies in Human Time*, trans. Elliott Coleman (Baltimore and London: Johns Hopkins University Press, 1956).

Reade, Winwood. *The Martyrdom of Man* (London: Watts, 1924).

Richards, I. A. *The Screens and Other Poems* (New York: Harcourt, Brace, 1960).

Shelley, Percy Bysshe. *Shelley's Prose in the Bodleian Manuscripts*, ed. A. H. Koszul (London: Frowde, 1910).

Shiel, M. P. *Science, Life and Literature* (London: Williams & Norgate, 1950).

Snow, C. P. *The Two Cultures: and A Second Look* (New York: Mentor, 1964).

Soddy, Frederick. *The Interpretation of Radium*, 3rd edn. (London: Murray, 1912).

Spengler, Oswald. *The Decline of the West*, trans. Charles Francis Atkinson (New York: Modern Library, 1962).

Stapledon, Olaf. *Last and First Men* and *Last Men in London* (Harmondsworth: Penguin, 1962).

Suvin, Darko. *Metamorphoses of Science Fiction* (New Haven and London: Yale University Press, 1979).

Suvin, Darko. *Positions and Presuppositions in Science Fiction* (Basingstoke: Macmillan, 1988).

Toffler, Alvin. *Future Shock* (London: Pan, 1971).

Wagar, W. Warren. *A Short History of the Future*, 2nd edn (London: Adamantine Press, 1992).

Wagar, W. Warren. *Terminal Visions: The Literature of Last Things* (Bloomington: Indiana University Press, 1982).

Waddington, C. H. *The Scientific Attitude*, 2nd edn (West Drayton: Penguin, 1948).

Weinberg, Steven. *The First Three Minutes: A Modern View of the Origin of the Universe* (London: Deutsch, 1977).

Werskey, Gary. *The Visible College: A Collective Biography of British Scientists and Socialists of the 1930s* (London: Free Association, 1988).

Westfahl, Gary. ' "The Jules Verne, H. G. Wells and Edgar Allan Poe Type of Story": Hugo Gernsback's History of Science Fiction', *Science-Fiction Studies* 58 (November 1992), pp. 340–53.

White, Hayden. *Metahistory: The Historical Imagination in Nineteenth-Century Europe* (Baltimore: Johns Hopkins University Press, 1973).

Zamyatin, Yevgeny. *A Soviet Heretic: Essays*, trans. Mirra Ginsburg (Chicago and London: University of Chicago Press, 1970).

Zamyatin, Yevgeny. *We*, trans. Bernard Guilbert Guerney (London: Cape, 1970).

Index